THINK SMARTER WITH NEMONIK THINKING

Third Edition

Dr. Auke Schade

nemonik-thinking.org

Copyright

Third Edition
Published 1 July 2016
@ nemonik-thinking.org
ISBN 978-0-473-29312-3

Abstract

This is the operating manual for your mind that you should have received at birth. Nemonik thinking is a smarter way of thinking that aims to maximize your success by evaluating seventeen nemoniks, which are memorized keywords describing all the perceived aspects of your mind, reality, and their interaction. Success is obtaining what you seek and escaping what you suffer. Therefore, it is goal oriented. To maximize your success, nemonik thinking mobilizes your hidden genius, accelerates your thinking, improves your memory, reveals opportunities and threats, creates questions and ideas, and reduces your stress levels. It is like playing a musical keyboard with seventeen keys producing an infinite repertoire of smart strategies. Nemonik thinking is unique because it is the first exhaustive and transferable way of thinking. Comparisons with Sir Richard Branson's way of thinking show that it is extremely productive. Unfortunately, the educational system conditions students still with pass-fail grades to win. Winning is defeating opponents in competition. Therefore, it is conflict oriented. The compulsion to win inhibits the truth and, therefore, fosters the corrupted way of conventional thinking. Conventional thinking creates the malignant cognitive virus CS7. In turn, that virus consolidates conventional thinking with cognitive dissonance and groupthink. Conventional thinking is time consuming. Hence, the less time you have, the greater the necessity to study nemonik thinking. You might be the best thinker in the world, but only nemonik thinking could make you the smartest thinker you can be.

nemonik-thinking.org

Dr. Auke Schade

My life started during the devastation of World War II. As a teenager, I worked as a carpenter and studied building engineering at night school. During the seventies, I became a financial manager for a multinational corporation, ran my own business, and studied economics in my spare time. My interest in the psychology of management extended to the interaction between the mind, body, and reality. In 1980, I immigrated to New Zealand where I obtained a doctorate in psychology from the University of Auckland. My mission is to make people the smartest thinkers they can be, which has led me to the development of nemonik thinking.[i]

Reality shows that humanity's way of thinking is failing dramatically. As a result, the next generation is facing overpopulation, dwindling resources, nuclear warfare, industrial pollution, climate change, etc. Therefore, they have to become the best thinkers they can be.

i Appendix: Nemonik Thinking.

Notes

CONTENTS

UNDERSTANDING NEMONIK THINKING

Nemonik thinking is an exhaustive and systematic way of thinking that maximizes the probability of success by subjecting seventeen nemoniks to both rational and affectorial thinking.

The problem

Blessed with ignorance, we call ourselves *Homo sapiens*, or *Wise humans*. Despite that self-assumed wisdom, reality shows that we are not doing well. We are facing huge global problems including overpopulation, diminishing resources, and pollution. Like falling dominos, those problems create a long string of threats such as climate change, deforestation, economic instability, empty oceans, nuclear war, poverty, terrorism, warfare, etc. As a result, humanity has become an endangered species and your future is in immediate danger. Nevertheless, there is only one underlying cause. Reality shows that all those problems are manmade, which supports my claim that our conventional way of thinking is failing. Ironically, that is a good thing because you can do something about it. Just become the best nemonik thinker you can be.

It stands to reason that no problems can be solved with the same way of thinking that has created them. Therefore, yesterday's solutions have become today's problems, while today's solutions will become tomorrow's problems. Seen the quantity and magnitude of our social and individual problems, our way of thinking has to be upgraded dramatically. That upgrade should focus on how we think, rather than what we think. If we solve our internal problems, then the external problems will disappear.

We are in this together because personal success is senseless if humanity fails. Even if you could escape in a spaceship, then you would still fail because you carry the virus of conventional thinking with you. Wherever you go, you would inevitably recreate the same problems you tried to escape. You can only succeed if you become the smartest thinker you can be. If you have a better plan, then let me know because we are running out of time. Nature is banging on our door.

The solution

Our common language is too ambiguous to describe the way we think. Definitions associated with the mind and reality are inherently hypothetical, fuzzy, and intertwined. It seems that neither the mind nor reality can be divided into distinct and precise components. Everything seems to work together in a holistic network. Nevertheless, to improve our understanding of the way we think, we have to identify, differentiate, and define those fuzzy components as good as possible. Therefore, I have redefined some common concepts and added new ones.[1]

Nemonik thinking is an exhaustive and systematic way of thinking that maximizes the probability of success by subjecting seventeen nemoniks to both rational and affectorial thinking. Thinking is a self-organizing mental process that recalls, evaluates, transforms, and generates information. In contrast, memory is a self-organising and associative mental process that stores, maintains, and recalls information in order to preserve it across space and time. We can memorize without thinking, but we cannot think without memorizing. Rational thinking is based on reason and logic, while affectorial thinking is associated with creativity, emotions, and intuitions. Although nemonik thinking is beneficial for your mental health, it is not a cure for mental illness. For such problems, you should follow the advice of your healthcare professional.

Nemoniks are seventeen memorized keywords describing the exhaustive aspects of the mind, reality, and the interaction of the mind and reality. Reality includes the phenomena surrounding the mind. The four mental nemoniks include the *objective, collective, creative, and the reactive mindmodes.* The nine reality nemoniks include *advance, stay, retreat, accumulate, preserve, dispose, act, wait, and prepare.* The four interactive nemoniks include *accept, reject, reveal, and conceal.* Furthermore, the thirteen operational nemoniks comprise the already mentioned nine reality nemoniks and the four interactive nemoniks. Together, those seventeen nemoniks comprise the nemonik template. The nemonik template is exhaustive, because it includes all possible aspects of thinking determined by the mind, reality, and their interaction. Nevertheless, the question remains—How could seventeen ordinary words improve significantly your thinking?

Right now, there is nothing special about those seventeen keywords. They are hardly mysterious because you knew them already. Of course—they cannot improve your thinking! Knowing those words without understanding their special meaning is as useless as knowing Albert Einstein's formula $E = mc^2$ without understanding the meaning of those letters. Although his formula holds the key to the awesome nuclear powers, if you do not know what E, m, and c stand for, that formula is utterly meaningless.[2] Similarly, just knowing the nemoniks without understanding their meaning will not make any difference to your thinking. That would be like having icons on your mobile without downloading the associated applications. You could tap those icons on the screen forever, but nothing would happen. This manual will help you to change those seventeen ordinary words into powerful cognitive tools.

The word nemonik is a phonetic notation of the Greek word mnemonic, which means *memory aid*. In accord, remembering the nemoniks will improve your memory by defragmentation. Defragmentation is the reorganization of separated information into united information. It is like organizing a random pile of books into a systematic library. After that organization, all the books about a particular nemonik will be stored on the same shelf. If you know the particular nemonik, then you have to search only one shelf instead of seventeen. Hence, defragmentation will accelerate the efficient storage, maintenance, and recall of information by a factor seventeen. Not a bad payback for learning just seventeen words.

Nature designed your memory to jump automatically from one concept to another associated concept. For example, using the word *kitchen* as a mnemonic might remind you of the dirty dishes in the sink—while they remind you of last night's party—which might lead you to think about your best friend etc. Each association occurs automatically and will release the next link in an endless chain of information. In the same way, each remembered nemonik prompts the memory to recall chains of information that are associated with that particular nemonik. Hence, the nemoniks changes the haphazard free-association of your memory into an efficient guided-association. Hence, your memory will become far more efficient.

The seventeen nemoniks are organic because they are like mental seeds growing towards your needs. Once planted, your memory will continuously attach more associated information to each nemonik. Ultimately, these seeds will become magnificent trees, which overshadow the little weeds in your mental garden. Your goals and priorities will become clear because the important things will stand out in your mind, while the trivial ones will disappear into the background. Hence, if you want to maximize your success, then it is in your interest to plant and nurture those seventeen nemoniks.

Nemoniks are more than simple mnemonics. The nemonik memory is no longer a passive library, but it guides and accelerates the process of thinking with the memorized nemoniks. The recalled nemoniks inform the mind what it should think about, while the memory provides strings of associated information for each nemonik. Consequently, nemonik thinking is the first true synthesis between memory and thinking.

Unpredictability is a strength. In accord, nemonik thinkers follow Lao Zi's advice—*Competent strategists have no strategy*. Instead, they create strategies and tactics that fit the particular situation. Nemoniks are their building blocks for strategical thinking, because they reveal strengths, weaknesses, threats, and opportunities that are associated with the actual situation. By recalling a nemonik, they prompt consciously their larger subconscious to generate ideas and reveal intuitions.

Each problem can be reduced to the nemonik template. Therefore, recalling that template provides immediately a cognitive checklist of seventeen keywords. This improves your thinking by reducing the probability of mental blind-spots. The nemonik template will also provide a preparedness that will decrease your stress levels and increases your self-confidence during emergencies. The nemonik template will accelerate your thinking and help you to think on your feet. You will know immediately what to do.

Lao Zi (570-490 BC) was a Chinese sage and philosopher who wrote about two-and-half thousand years ago the book *Dao De Jing.*[3] Nemonik thinking incorporates Lao Zi's definition of success—*Obtain what you seek and escape what you suffer.* His definition sounds simple. However, his words should never be taken at face value. He was one of the great ancient thinkers and there are many layers of understanding to his writings.[ii]

Despite Lao Zi's advice, some people try to obtain what they suffer most, while others try to escape what they need most. You are likely to get what you ask for, but you might not appreciate what you asked for. For example, if you do not like the current industrial global warming, then you might desire a normal climate. Would that not be nice? May be not! That normal climate freezes this planet 90% of the time.[iii] On the other hand, if you ask for nothing, then you will get nothing. Hence, setting beneficial goals is the first and most crucial step towards success. Do not worry. If you cannot find a goal, then you might be looking too hard—relax and follow your passion. Do what you like to do most, because true success is measured in the heart, rather than in the head. The feeling of success is emotional, rather than rational. Ultimately, you can only feel successful if your goals please your heart.[4]

Although in our common language, the difference between winning and success might be trivial, that difference is crucial for improving your thinking. The aim of conventional think-

---

[ii] Appendix: Lao Zi's Dao De Jing

[iii] Appendix: Global Warming...

ing is to maximize the probability of winning. Winning is defeating opponents in competition and, therefore, winning is conflict oriented, which fosters control, force, aggression, enemies, and win-lose strategies. In contrast, nemonik thinking aims to maximize the probability of success and, therefore, it is goal oriented, which fosters freedom, alignment, compassion, allies, and win-win strategies. Compassion is the affectorial sympathy for other people that inhibits competitive behaviour in order to maximize the collective probability of success.

Nemonik thinkers will not waste their time and effort on winning unproductive and ego-stroking competitions. No matter who wins, both competitors will inevitably weaken because they will lose resources during the competition. When their combined resources are reduced, a third party might use their weakness as an opportunity to defeat them. In accord, Sun Zi, the warrior of all warriors, wrote in *The Art of War—Competent generals do not fight.*[iv] If you have to fight, then you have already made tactical and strategical blunders. Hence, nemonik thinkers are very reluctant to fight. However, that avoidance does not mean that they are do-gooders. They are strategists who position themselves continuously to maximize their success. They prefer to take the undamaged resources from their opponents by positioning themselves, rather than fighting for them. Nevertheless, if they are forced to fight, then they are likely to win, because they use nemonik thinking. Hence, maximizing the probability of success is more productive than maximizing the probability of winning.

Nemonik thinking is the new operating system for the brain. In computer terminology, an operating system is the basic software that tells a set of electronic components how to act as a computer.[5] Similarly, nemonik thinking tells the neurons in the brain how to act as a thinker. Nemonik thinking will maximize your success because it is pragmatic, mobilizes your hidden genius, accelerates your thinking, improves

---

[iv] Appendix: Sun Zi's Art...

your memory, turns your weaknesses into strengths, reveals opportunities and threats, and prepares you for emergencies. Nemonik thinking is the first way of thinking that can be transferred from one person to another and from one generation to the next.

Best of all, you do not have to worry about the application of nemonik thinking. Once you have consciously memorized the nemoniks, your subconscious will habituate automatically nemonik thinking. Trust me—your mind is amazing. Nemonik thinking is the solution, because it will make you the smartest thinker you can be. All it takes is seventeen words!

Nemonik Thinking

Nemonik thinking is an exhaustive and systematic way of thinking that maximizes the probability of success by subjecting seventeen nemoniks to rational and affectorial thinking. Nemonik thinking aims to maximize the probability of success and, therefore, it is goal oriented, which fosters freedom, alignment, compassion, allies, and win-win strategies.

Notes

Table 01 illustrates that nemonik thinking includes the mind, reality, and the interaction between mind and reality. Those aspects are exhaustive and will be discussed in the following sections. Just stay with me, it might get exciting!

Table 01: Parts of nemonik thinking

Nemonik thinking			
Mind			
	Conscious		
		Rational thinking	
			OBJECTIVE-1
			COLLECTIVE-2
	Subconscious		
		Affectorial thinking	
			CREATIVE-3
			REACTIVE-4
Reality			
		Space	
			ADVANCE-5
			STAY-6
			RETREAT-7
		Matter	
			ACCUMULATE-8
			PRESERVE-9
			DISPOSE-10
		Time	
			ACT-11
			WAIT-12
			PREPARE-13
Interaction			
		Perception	
			ACCEPT-14
			REJECT-15
		Projection	
			REVEAL-16
			CONCEAL-17

MIND

The mind is the nonmaterial part of a person that comprises the total of all conscious, subconscious, and semiconscious mental structures and processes. The mind is abstract, because you cannot see, hear, taste, smell, or touch the mind. The mind is a theoretical construct that exists paradoxically only in the mind. Nevertheless, this elusive construct helps us to evaluate our way of thinking. Furthermore, mindware is a hypothetical set of nonmaterial self-organizing processes that creates and maintains the mind. Mindware could be compared to the software of a computer. On the other hand, brainware is a set of self-organizing organic components and processes that support the mindware. In computer terminology, brainware could be compared to the hardware of a computer. Although brainware seems to be wired initially by nature, it has to change in some way in order to think and memorize.

A healthy mind features a will to maximize success, abilities to think and memorize, and a reliable and valid interaction with the surrounding reality. A tenet of nemonik thinking is that the reality shapes the mind with rewards and punishments. This forces people to think in terms of that reality and, therefore, the mind can only be understood within the context of that reality. Understanding reality is understanding the mind.

The external reality comprises material and immaterial phenomena that surround the mind. That reality presents a gigantic and constant stream of information to the mind. As a result, the mind has to process sounds, images, aromas, flavours, temperatures, and pressures. It has to process, store, maintain, and recall this information, while simultaneously processing ideas, beliefs, emotions, and intuitions. On top of that, it has to make decisions and act. It has also to regulate many physiological processes.

If you would be consciously aware of all the cognitive processes, then you would be unable to focus on anything.

There would be just too much raw information. It would be like a computer displaying all its stored information in a fast and chaotic stream—mixing up all your programs, videos, pictures, music, and text. You would be unable to make any sense of that chaos. This huge stream would cause an information overload, which is the counterproductive awareness of processing consciously too much information.

Nature prevents a cognitive information overload by dividing the mind in a small conscious and a large subconscious. The conscious comprises the information that is relevant to the actual situation at hand. On the other hand, the subconscious comprises the information that is irrelevant to the actual situation. In computer terminology, the conscious is similar to the Randomly Accessible Memory (RAM), while the subconscious is similar to the hard-drive of a computer.

CONSCIOUS

The conscious is a small part of the mind that is only active when a person is fully awake. The conscious is associated with awareness, concentration, learning, Self, reality, and rational thinking. Conscious dominance is a healthy mental state that is fostered by concentration. A mental state is a distinct level of awareness. During conscious dominance, the conscious is active, while the conscious awareness of subconscious activity is inhibited. The aim of conscious dominance includes focussing on the actual situation, learning new tasks, providing direction, and managing the subconscious. Concentration is an intentional mental process that fosters conscious dominance by focusing consciously on a particular aspect of the sensory reality in order to inhibit unintentional conscious thoughts. The Self is the observer of a person's internal reality, which that person consciously calls 'I'.[6] The Self of a healthy person is projected to the reality through a set of stable behavioural and mental characteristics. The essence of the Self is elusive because it tends to disappear when one tries to study it. Nevertheless, it is holistic because it is appears in every part of the mind. The conscious is like the small visible part of an iceberg, while the subconscious is the larger submerged part.

SUBCONSCIOUS

The subconscious is the large part of the mind that is continuously active outside the conscious awareness of that person. The prime aim of the subconscious is to protect the conscious from an information overload. The subconscious is associated with sleep, dreaming, relaxation, knowledge, genius, internal reality, and affecters.

Affecters are mental signals that are generated by subconscious affectorial thinking, which influence the conscious without explaining the underlying subconscious processes. Affecters include beliefs, desires, discoveries, emotions, fantasies, habits, heuristics, ideas, impulses, innovations, insights, inspirations, intuitions, inventions, novelties, reactions, reflexes, routines, skills, etc. Affecters do not rely on conscious reasoning or facts and, therefore, they are by definition non-rational and illogical. However, affecters are sometimes rationalised. Rationalizing is a corrupted version of rational thinking that provides pseudo-rational justifications to defend a previously made conclusion. Rationalization is a conscious rational attempt to understand and justify the non-rational subconscious.

The acquisition of information cost much time and effort. Therefore, the information stored in the subconscious is precious. Whether correct or incorrect, the subconscious will protect the acquired information against opposing information with groupthink and cognitive dissonance.

Gullible people change their minds all the time.
Stubborn people change their minds never.
Nemonik thinkers change their minds to fit the actual situation.

Groupthink is a collective mental process rejecting correct information in order to protect incorrect information that is already accepted by that collective as true. Members will coerce each other to comply with the group doctrine. Tools of groupthink are social rewards and punishment, peer pressure, ostracizing, labelling, ridicule, and aggression. Groupthink provides stability and prevents erratic changes in the collective. However, groupthink could backfire and become counterproductive for the collective by fostering mental stagnation. Therefore, each collective needs a devil's advocate who rattles the cage and will make the members revaluate their beliefs. This prevents that the collective develops tunnel vision and that members conform to unrealistic ideas. Literally, *the devil's advocate* is an official who puts the case against beatification or canonization. In daily life, it is the person who always defends the opposite side.

Cognitive dissonance is an individual mental process rejecting correct information in order to protect the incorrect information that is already accepted by the subconscious of that individual as true. In order to block the incoming information, the subconscious sends negative affecters to the conscious such as anxiety, frustration, and aggression. Cognitive dissonance provides mental stability and prevents erratic changes in the thinking of the individual. However, cognitive dissonance could backfire and become counterproductive for the individual by fostering mental stagnation.

The overload protection implies that the subconscious creates a genius by accumulating knowledge and skills that are hidden from the conscious. Therefore, your conscious understanding of reality might lag behind your subconscious understanding. You might subconsciously know things that you do not know or understand consciously. This mental paradox is named—*knowing without knowing, mind without mind, or thinking without thinking.* Hence, the overload protection of the conscious creates the basis for your intuition.

Subconscious dominance is a healthy mental state that is fostered by relaxation. During this state, the subconscious is active, while the conscious is inhibited. The aim of this state is mental and physical recuperation.

Relaxation is a mental process that fosters subconscious dominance by inhibiting involuntary conscious thoughts.

Some people might point out that they have hobbies or play sports in order to relax. However, that is recreation, rather than relaxation. Recreation is the intentional replacement of activities that are essential for success with nonessential ones. Hence, if you are a professional golfer, then playing golf is essential for your success. If you play golf as a friendly game, then it is a nonessential activity or recreation. Recreation is different from relaxation, because recreation might involve awareness, effort, focus, learning, reason, vigilance, etc. In addition, recreation does not aim to evoke subconscious dominance or sleep. Nevertheless, some recreation such as chanting, dancing, drumming, and walking might evoke semiconscious dominance. More about that in the next section.

SEMICONSCIOUS

The semiconscious is a part of the mind that comprises parts of the conscious and subconscious, which form a communication channel between those parts of the mind. Semiconscious dominance is a healthy mental state that is fostered by meditation. This state fosters conscious awareness of subconscious activity and the conscious improvement of the subconscious way of affectorial thinking. Semiconscious dominance is associated with dream awareness, meditation, hypnosis, and drowsiness. Dreaming is a subconscious process that updates the brain and mind with information that was collected during conscious dominance. The awareness of dreaming is semiconscious because you have to be consciously aware of that subconscious process.[v]

Meditation is an intentional mental process that fosters concentration on relaxation. Meditation fosters semicon-

---

[v] Appendix: Dreaming.

scious dominance by focusing consciously on a particular aspect of the internal reality, which inhibits unintentional conscious thoughts. A person in meditation maintains a delicate balance between conscious and subconscious dominance. Meditation seems to create a mysterious sanctuary deep within the mind, where the concepts of time, space, and matter become blurred.

Many practitioners of meditation try to escape reality. Some seek enlightenment or the eternal truth, while others aim for a close contact with divine entities. Whatever they seek or try to escape, they reach a beneficial state of mind that is characterized by feelings of bliss, contentment, ecstasy, enjoyment, euphoria, happiness, and peace. Meditation provides relaxation and hope during times of stress and despair.

Meditation is a beneficial tool for managing your physical and mental well-being. This includes anxiety, blood pressure, concentration, conflict resolution, creativity, decision making, determination, enlightenment, exam preparation, headaches, memory, mindpower, pain management, panic resistance, problem solving, relaxation, self-confidence, sleep, study, thinking, vascular health, etc. Although this list is far from complete, it would surprise me if none of these items would be on your wish-list.

Meditation fosters a silent mind, which is a mental state that is devoid of conscious thoughts and fosters subconscious action without conscious interference. A silent mind does not mean ignorance. A silent mind is a mental state during which the conscious is pure, tranquil, and at rest. The silent mind is also called the *empty mind* or the *zone*. However, the mind is silent, rather than empty.

Nemonik meditation is a special type of meditation that uses visualizations and unvoiced mantras in order to improve affecters during semiconscious dominance. Nemonik meditation integrates auto-balance, breathing, conditioning, mantras, meditation, positive affirmations, progressive relaxation, relaxation, and visualizations. Auto-balance is the dynamic balance between the state of the mind and the state of the body, which moves on a continuum ranging from tension to relaxation. A mantra is a repeated voiced or unvoiced phrase, word, or sound that fosters semiconscious dominance by inhibiting unintentional conscious thoughts. A positive affirmation is a mantra that improves the subconscious e.g.—Each day I feel better. Progressive relaxation was introduced by Edmund Jacobson (1888-1983). It is a conscious and systematic process of alternating tension and relaxation of the muscles. Furthermore, a visualization is a mental picture that is consciously maintained in the mind in order to inhibit unintentional conscious thoughts during mediation.

Hypnosis is a mental process initiated by a hypnotist who voices suggestions to evoke semiconscious dominance in the subject. During that semiconscious dominance, the hypnotists voices suggestions to change the subconscious of the subject. After completing the changes, the hypnotist voices suggestions to restore conscious dominance. The suggestions to change the subconscious of the subject remain effective after the subject is woken up by the hypnotist.[vi]

The strength of the suggestions in nemonik meditation and hypnosis depends on the depth of the semiconscious dominance. The practitioner of nemonik mediation has to reach a state of semiconscious dominance, while maintaining enough conscious dominance to deliver the suggestions to the subconscious. On the other hand, a hypnotist can evoke a deeper semiconscious dominance in the subject, because the subject does not have to remain conscious to deliver the suggestions. Therefore, hypnosis might be more effective. However, you should be extremely careful to hand over control of your precious mind to another person. After all, a hypnotist could induce counterproductive post-hypnotic suggestions.

Unconscious

Unconsciousness is an unhealthy mental state that is characterized by a persistent unawareness of reality and the Self.

[vi] Appendix: Hypnosis

Unconsciousness differs from subconscious dominance, because the unconscious person will not wake up voluntarily in case of danger. Hence, unconsciousness could be seen as a suspension of life. Nevertheless, the mind might still aim to restore the normal conscious and subconscious activities. Unconsciousness could be caused by physical or mental traumas, analgesics, asphyxiation, and toxic substances.

Table 02: Parts of the mind

Nemonik thinking
  Mind
    Conscious
      Rational thinking
        OBJECTIVE-1
        COLLECTIVE-2
    Subconscious
      Affectorial thinking
        CREATIVE-3
        REACTIVE-4
  Reality
      Space
        ADVANCE-5
        STAY-6
        RETREAT-7
      Matter
        ACCUMULATE-8
        PRESERVE-9
        DISPOSE-10
      Time
        ACT-11
        WAIT-12
        PREPARE-13
  Interaction
      Perception
        ACCEPT-14
        REJECT-15
      Projection
        REVEAL-16
        CONCEAL-17

Table 02 illustrates that the conscious and subconscious are the exhaustive parts of the mind. The semiconscious is not shown in the table because it is part of the conscious and subconscious.

Although introspection suggests that we have a conscious, semiconscious, and subconscious, the descriptions of those concepts are inherently fuzzy. It might be that the semiconscious is a transitional layer in a mental continuum ranging from conscious to subconscious extremes. In that case, there are no clear distinctions. Nevertheless, that would not make much difference for the structure of nemonik thinking. The mind is like a brilliant rainbow—there are no clear distinctions between its colours. Nevertheless, we perceive different colours and, similarly, also different layers of the mind.

Exercise

Before reading the following sections, you are invited to complete the exercise in appendix: Exercise WWI (Part I). The aim is to provide information about your cognitive skills before and after reading this manual.

BILATERAL THINKING

Table 03 illustrates that the conscious generates rational thinking to deal with the perceived order of reality, while the larger subconscious generates affectorial thinking to deal with the perceived chaos of reality. Hence, nemonik thinking is a bilateral way of thinking. Nevertheless, concentration and relaxation inhibit each other. As a result, conscious rational thinking inhibits subconscious affectorial thinking and vice versa. This mutual inhibition has important consequences for your way of thinking.

Table 03: Main ways of thinking				
Nemonik thinking				
	Mind			
		Conscious		
			Rational thinking	
				OBJECTIVE-1
				COLLECTIVE-2
		Subconscious		
			Affectorial thinking	
				CREATIVE-3
				REACTIVE-4
	Reality			
			Space	
				ADVANCE-5
				STAY-6
				RETREAT-7
			Matter	
				ACCUMULATE-8
				PRESERVE-9
				DISPOSE-10
			Time	
				ACT-11
				WAIT-12
				PREPARE-13
	Interaction			
			Perception	
				ACCEPT-14
				REJECT-15
			Projection	
				REVEAL-16
				CONCEAL-17

Edward Lorenz (1917-2008) was an American mathematician and meteorologist who introduced *Chaos Theory.*[7] Order is the part of the external reality that can be subjected to reason. It is associated with comprehensibility, knowledge, predictability, recognisability, etc. In contrast, chaos is the part of the external reality that cannot be subjected to reason. It is associated with incomprehensibility, belief, predictability, unrecognizability, etc.

Lorenz argued that the universe is a deterministic system, but that small differences in the initial conditions cause unpredictable outcomes or chaos. He called this—*The Butterfly Effect*, because the wing beat of a tiny butterfly might create a powerful tornado. Please, do not breathe too deeply—you might disturb the atmosphere.

Herbert Spencer (1820-1903) was an English philosopher who emphasized the important distinctions between the *known, unknown,* and *unknowable.*[8] Acquiring knowledge transforms chaos into order—it changes Spencer's *unknown* into the *known.*[9] Hence, the distinction between order and chaos depends on the development of one's mind, rather than on immutable features of reality. Therefore, order and chaos are subjective concepts.

Order comprises predictable phenomena such as the seasons, while chaos comprises unpredictable phenomena such as lightning. Our ancestors were forced to cope with both the predictable and unpredictable aspects of reality long before Lorenz' chaos theory came about. During that evolution, the mind of the survivors developed rational thinking to deal with the order of reality and affectorial thinking to deal with the chaos of reality.

Rational thinking

The Greek philosopher Aristotle (384-322 BC) assumed that there is order in reality and, therefore, that reality is predictable and subject to rational thinking. Rational thinking is the conscious part of nemonik thinking that deals with the predictable order of reality by submitting facts to reason in order to create new facts. Facts are testable descriptions of reality that are supported adequately by sensory perception and reason. Sensory perception is the perception by the senses of material signals that are emitted by reality.

Reason comprises formal logic and informal logic. Formal logic is a part of reason that submits facts to validity rules in order to evaluate the truth of logical arguments and draw true conclusions, which become new facts. Informal logic is a part of reason that is based on former formal logic that has been transformed into aphorisms. Aphorisms include folk wisdoms, heuristics, rules of thumb, truisms, clichés, definitions, mottos, and proverbs. Informal logic is efficient and provides instantaneously a fit for the actual situation.

The mental processes of rational thinking are within the conscious awareness and, therefore, they can be observed and communicated. Aristotle's writings about logic were compiled by the Peripatetics under the name *Organon* or *Instrument.*

A logical argument is the part of formal logic that contains a set of facts leading to an irrefutable conclusion that becomes a new fact. For example, imagine an elephant (E) that is larger than a dog (D), which is larger than a mouse (M). This could be written as (E > D) and (D > M).[vii] Those facts would then lead to the irrefutable conclusion that (E > M). Even if you have never seen an animal, you know from that logical argument that an elephant is larger than a mouse. Hence, logic could help if you were a zookeeper.

[vii] Larger than (>). Smaller than (<).

A true logical argument is consistent, reliable, and valid. A consistent argument features a strong connection between the facts (D is a common factor in the facts E > D and D > M). A reliable argument comprises only facts (E should be indeed larger than D, while D should be indeed larger than M). A valid argument comprises facts that are related to the conclusion that they intend to support. If (Z) would be a zebra, then the conclusion E > Z would be invalid, because Z is not associated with the given facts E > D and D > M. The conclusion might be true, but it is not supported by logic because it is an invalid argument.

Fortunately, the application of formal logic extends beyond the comparison of animals. Every day, we use it in one way or another—we could not survive without it. Furthermore, all computers use formal logic. They would not exist without Aristotle's ideas. For example, the previous argument could be written in computer code (If E is larger than D; and D is larger than M; then E is larger than M). Given the facts, even a computer could tell you that an elephant is larger than a mouse. Nevertheless, that computer could still not tell you whether the elephant is larger than the zebra (E > Z?).

Not every description of reality is a fact. For example, a hypothesis is a testable description of reality that has not yet been subjected to reason. Hypotheses include assumptions, postulations, presumptions, tenets, theories, etc. For example, a child might test the hypothesis that an egg bounces when it falls on the concrete. This hypothesis could be accepted as a fact if there is adequate evidence that the egg bounces, or alternatively, it could be rejected if the evidence is insufficient and the egg breaks. In all likelihood, that test would be a waste of a good omelette. As you see, true knowledge never comes cheap.

Furthermore, a belief is the acceptance of an untestable description of reality. For example, a belief in an alternative universe cannot be tested (yet) and, therefore, it is neither a fact nor a hypothesis. The core of any belief is the absence of rational testability and evidence. Therefore, a belief cannot be justified with the logic of rational thinking. If a belief is testable then it becomes automatically a hypothesis and if there is adequate evidence then it becomes a fact. People who need evidence for their belief have by definition a weak belief. Beliefs are associated with canons, creeds, doctrines, dogmas, faiths, ideologies, religions, etc.

Ancient mythology was our first attempt to explain the unpredictable chaos of reality. In Greek mythology, Zeus represented the chaos of reality. Everything that could not be predicted or explained was attributed to the Gods on the Olympus. Aristotle's ideas broke the hold of mythology on the mind as the major source of explaining chaos. His reason changed irreversibly our mental and physical world. Reason replaced mythology. Not many believe still that Zeus determines what will happen to them. However, Aristotelian reason describes the order of reality, while mythology describes the chaos of reality. Therefore, Aristotelian reason and ancient mythology are not mutually exclusive. They describe different aspects of the same dualistic reality—different sides of the same coin.

Aristotle used logic to discover the natural order and truth, which is the basis of modern physics. His ideas are still crucial for our development, because without his *if...then...* statements we would have no computers, mobile phones, or internet. He wrote the first operating system for the brain and the computer. Now, many believe in the infallibility of computers that rely purely on Aristotelian logic. However, not many understand or are able to test the reason that is hidden within their computers. Hence, Aristotelian logic has become a new mythology in which computers have replaced the deities, and programmers replaced the priesthood.

Rational thinkers think consciously and, therefore, they can explain their thinking to someone else. This fosters mutual understanding and communication. The objectivity of a logical argument about facts is likely to synthesize different descriptions of reality, while the emotions released by a heated debate about subjective beliefs might drive people apart.

Affectorial thinking

Affectorial thinking is the subconscious part of nemonik thinking that deals with the unpredictable chaos of reality by generating affecters that influence the conscious. As mentioned previously, affecters are mental signals that are generated by subconscious affectorial thinking, which influence the conscious without explanations. Affecters include beliefs, common sense, desires, discoveries, emotions, fantasies, feelings, habits, heuristics, ideas, impulses, innovations, insights, inspirations, intuitions, inventions, novelties, reactions, reflexes, routines, sensibility, skills, etc.

Affectorial thinking is non-rational. It is a subconscious way of thinking and, therefore, the underlying mental processes are outside the conscious awareness. You cannot consciously apply reason to those processes. Therefore, it appears non-rational to the rational conscious. In order to apply affectorial thinking, one has to trust unconditionally the truth of the affecters. That requires trust in your Self, which is associated with positive features such as self-confidence and charisma, but also with negative features such as arrogance, close mindedness, unrealism, and gullibility.

You could apply reality-checks in order to reduce the negative effects of trusting your Self. A reality-check is a critical evaluation with rational thinking whether a particular affecter fits reality. However, there is a threat that the check becomes a rationalization of a counterproductive affecter. Despite many advantages of rational thinking, the most precious things in life, such as art, creativity, beauty, happiness, and love are the results of affectorial thinking. Rational thinking seems to keep us alive in order to enjoy the non-rational affecters.

The systematic approach of nemonik thinking seems to favour rational thinking. However, nemonik thinking is a bilateral way of thinking. The structure of nemonik thinking is a precious balance between rational and non-rational affectorial thinking—a balance between the reason of the head and the passion of the heart. There is no best way of thinking. It all depends on the situation. Therefore, you will need both ways in order to become the smartest thinker you can be.

Sir Richard's mental bias

Sir Richard mentioned that he suffers from dyslexia. Dyslexia is an impairment in reading ability not resulting from low intelligence. He explains that dyslexia forces him to rely on his intuitions and gut feelings, rather than on detailed facts and figures.[10] In terms of nemonik thinking, this suggests that he is involuntarily biased towards affectorial thinking and against rational thinking. In accord with Lao Zi, this bias could explain his success—*Learning many details (rational) is exhausting and not as good as following your heart (affectorial).*[11]

Sir Richard mentions that he hates to be controlled and that he thrives in chaos. For example, he disliked the controls that were imposed on him by the rational specialists from organizations such as Coutts' bank and the City.[12] Moreover, he seeks conditions where affectorial thinking is a necessity such as flying fragile balloons in high-speed jet streams. Those conditions are so chaotic that five out of seven people died in previous attempts to cross the Atlantic.[13] However, Sir Richard's mental bias towards affectorial thinking provides the optimal fit. Accuracy, creativity, efficiency, intuition, and fast decisions are more useful in such chaos than a 500-page manual that explains in rational terminology how to fly a balloon.

Sir Richard's mental bias towards affectorial thinking could lure some people into the trap of underestimating his rational thinking. Indeed, he admits that numbers in theoretical situations might confuse him, but he also mentions that numbers in practical situations make perfect sense to him. This is supported by his success in the competitive business world. He also loves to play the devil's advocate, which suggests that he likes the critical aspects of rational thinking. In addition, he recognizes his rational weakness and, therefore, he associates with people who compensate for it. Hence, his rational weakness is not a weakness anymore.[14] As Lao Zi points out—*Sages regard a weakness as a weakness; thus, it is not a weakness.*[15]

Sir Richard seems to have applied rational thinking when he reduced Virgin's huge debt by cutting the cost, aborting the takeover of EMI, and selling Virgin Music.[16] Although he did not want to sell Virgin Music. His rational thinking prevailed that time over his affectorial thinking. Otherwise, he might have lost Virgin Atlantic and damaged Virgin Music beyond repair.[17]

Apparently, the laws of aerodynamics predict that the bumblebee cannot fly—its body seems to be too large for its wings. However, the bumblebee ignores our predictions and keeps flying. Therefore, we have to review our understanding of aerodynamics. Similarly, Sir Richard's dyslexia has the potential to inhibit success in the rational business world. However, like the bumblebee, his success defies that prediction. Hence, we might have to rethink also the consequences of dyslexia.

If we ignore the mysticism of Zen, then some of its practices seem to strengthen non-rational thinking with koans. A koan is a riddle that has no conscious rational solution, which forces the conscious to listen to the non-rational subconscious. For example, a Zen master brings his hands together, while saying to a student—*This is the sound of two hands clapping. What is the sound of one hand clapping?*[18]

Zen practice is about inhibiting rational thinking, rather than solving the koan. Although it looks like a test, it is not a test and there might be many non-rational answers. The more you think about the koan, the more you foster non-rational thinking. If you find the 'solution', then you have also to find a new koan in order to keep exercising.

Sir Richard's dyslexia might have a similar effect as Zen practice. Both inhibit rational thinking and, therefore, foster non-rational affectorial thinking. This enhances creativity and personal perfection. Could it be that dyslexia is sometimes an advantage, rather than a disadvantage? Researchers should test the hypothesis that inhibiting rational thinking maximizes success by fostering affectorial thinking.

RATIONAL NEMONIKS

Natural and Artificial

Table 04 illustrates that the two exhaustive parts of rational thinking are the *objective and collective* mindmodes. The mental order generated by rational thinking deals with the order of reality. In his book *Dao De Jing,* Lao Zi was one of the first ancient philosophers to make a clear distinction between the natural and artificial order of reality. Natural refers to the part of reality that is not manmade, while artificial refers to the manmade part of reality. Lao Zi's concept of *Dao* is the way of nature.[19] To date, we would call that physics, which is thinking about the way that nature works. On the other hand, *De* is the way of people that we would now call psychology, which is thinking about the artificial way that people work.[20] In accord, rational thinking comprises the objective and collective mindmodes, which deal respectively with the natural and artificial order of reality. A mindmode is a specific way of thinking that deals with a specific aspect of reality.

Table 04: Rational nemoniks
Nemonik thinking
Mind
Conscious
Rational thinking
OBJECTIVE-1
COLLECTIVE-2
Subconscious
Affectorial thinking
CREATIVE-3
REACTIVE-4
Reality
Space
ADVANCE-5
STAY-6
RETREAT-7
Matter
ACCUMULATE-8
PRESERVE-9
DISPOSE-10
Time
ACT-11
WAIT-12
PREPARE-13
Interaction
Perception
ACCEPT-14
REJECT-15
Projection
REVEAL-16
CONCEAL-17

RATIONAL NEMONIK 1—OBJECTIVE

The objective mindmode is a way of rational thinking that deals with the natural order of reality, which can be described by natural laws and facts that make nature predictable. Objective refers to a description of reality that is independent of what anyone believes. Natural laws are objective descriptions of the unchangeable cause-effect relationships of nature or the laws of physics. Natural facts are unchangeable facts about nature. The objective mindmode uses the mental order of reason to deal with the natural order of reality.

Keywords for *objective* include: *data collection, experimentation, formal logic, hypothesis tests, literature reviews, mathematics, measurements, natural facts, natural laws, natural, peer review, rational thinking, reliability tests, replicated results, samples, science, scientific method, sensory observations, statistical analyses, testing, truth, validity tests, etc.*

Sir Isaac Newton (1642-1727) was a British mathematician and physicist. He was one of the first scientists to describe objectively the basic laws of nature in his book *Principia.*[21] The natural laws that prevail in daily life are always true and consistently enforced by nature. For example, gravity always causes all matter within a vacuum to fall towards other matter. Therefore, you can predict that your keys will fall to the ground. Otherwise, they could drift off into space and would be hard to find after a late night out. The cycles of day and night, the tides, and the seasons are also predictable. Therefore, farmers know when to plant and harvest. Unpredictable seasons would destroy their crops. Hence, the predictability of nature could help you to maximize your success. The supernatural is outside the scope of nemonik thinking.

The *Universal Law of Causality* prevails in daily life and holds that the same natural cause always precedes the same natural effect. In accord, no one has to enforce the laws or facts of nature because the response of nature is consistent and automatic. Furthermore, the objective mindmode has developed the scientific method. The scientific method is based on analyses, experimentation, data collection, formal logic, generalization, literature reviews, mathematics, measurements, natural laws, peer reviews, samples, sensory observations, reliability tests, replicated results, statistical analysis, hypothesis tests, validity tests, etc. The scientific method has supported the Industrial, Biotechnical, and Informational Revolutions.

The German philosopher Georg Wilhelm Friedrich Hegel (1770-1831) introduced a dialectic that describes the progress of scientific knowledge. That dialectic holds that each thesis evokes an antithesis, which is followed by a synthesis. A thesis is a potential description of reality, while an antithesis is a description of reality that contradicts the thesis. Furthermore, a synthesis is a description of reality that merges the thesis and antithesis into a new thesis. Hegel's dialectic is a process of successive approximation that supposedly leads to the objective truth. Successive approximation is a cyclic process that moves each turn closer towards the ultimate goal. Hegel's dialectic is the basis of the nemonik accelerator. The nemonik accelerator is a cognitive method that increases the speed of your thinking by fostering agreement during disagreement, while fostering disagreement during agreement.

Sir Richard's objective mindmode

The idea that Sir Richard is biased involuntarily against objective thinking is supported by his reported difficulties with mathematics and root learning, and his distrust of numbers, statistics, and academics.[22] Our society relies heavily on science and technology and, therefore, objective thinking is hard to avoid. However, if we need objective information, then we could let objective specialists think for us. For instance, objective programmers write the programs for our computers. Objective engineers translate the ideas of creative specialists into prototypes that are then copied by manufacturers. Objective chemists combine substances in order to develop and produce our medicines. The results of objective thinking can be used even if the user does not understand the working of the tools. Many people use computers, emails, and mobile phones, but only a few can explain the electronic details of these products. The consumers use objective devices without involving their objective mindmode. Sir Richard compensated for his bias against objective thinking by associating himself with objective specialists in airlines, ballooning, computer consumables, computer games, cosmetics, financial-services, railways, soft drinks, etc.[23]

RATIONAL NEMONIK 2—COLLECTIVE

The collective mindmode is a way of rational thinking that generates artificial rules, which determine the rights and obligations of individuals within a collective and makes their behaviours predictable. A collective is an organized group of people with a common goal such as a family, business, tribe, nation, or the entire human race. It is the aim of collectives to maximize their success. Therefore, they create a predictable order with artificial rules that govern the interactions between their members and between collectives. As you know, artificial refers to that part of reality that is manmade. Artificial rules are descriptions of the changeable cause-effect relationships that are only true within a particular collective, because they are based on decisions of that collective. They include criminal, civil, and commercial rules, agreements, consents, contracts, creeds, customs, doctrines, dogmas, morals, rituals, social agreements, traditions, treaties, etc. The collective mindmode uses the mental order of reason to deal with the artificial order of reality.

Keywords for *collective* include: *artificial, artificial facts, artificial rules, bureaucracy, conflict, conform, control, co-operation, criminals, efficient, enforcement, hierarchy, indoctrination, inequality, judiciary, law and order, law-making, negotiation, obligations, outlaws, social perfection, privileges, punishment, rational thinking, rebellion, revolution, reward, suppression, verdicts, etc.*

People are part of nature. However, their complex interactions generate an artificial way of collective thinking. The Chinese philosopher Confucius (551-479 BC) was one of the first ancient philosophers to address the problems concerning the artificial rules of collectives. After his death, his students compiled his ideas in a manuscript called *The Analects.*[24]

The members of a collective might agree not to steal from each other and not to kill each other. However, the collective could change such artificial rules and, therefore, the cause-effect relationship is changeable. Hence, artificial rules are only true within the particular collective. Nevertheless, ignoring artificial rules might have fatal consequences. In some countries, people have decided to drive on the right hand side of the road, while in other countries they drive on the left hand side. Hence, it is a rational but artificial fact that you have to drive on the correct side of the road in order to survive.

The effect of collective thinking is reaching deep into the human mind. The collective mindmode is even the mother of language. It produces artificial rules that determine the use of particular sounds and symbols for the description and differentiation of phenomena. Language becomes rational through agreement. It is the artificial glue that binds individuals to a collective. In that sense, nemonik thinking itself is a meta-language that could improve communication between people and between collectives. Furthermore, it might surprise you that even objective arithmetic is subject to collective rules. For example, calculate the answer for (2 + 5 x 7 = ?). It seems to be easy. Nevertheless, if you do not know the collective rules then you might make a mistake. I invite you to compare your answer with the endnote.[25] This shows that even arithmetic is not objective, but based on artificial collective rules. I you change the rules, then you change the outcome.

Hegel's dialectic is concerned with science, but the same dialectic occurs in the legal system in which the prosecutor and defence lawyer provide a thesis and antithesis. The judge delivers with his verdict the synthesis, which fosters the progress of legislation. Nevertheless, artificial rules are always subject to the natural laws. No collective can enforce the decision that pigs should fly or that the tide should stop. People could take advantage of the natural laws, but reality shows that ignoring them is counterproductive.

In terms of nature, we are weak. We have no large teeth, sharp claws, or a thick fur to protect ourselves. Our closest relative in nature, the chimpanzee, is about six times stronger! We cannot fly and many cannot even swim. Compared to other species, we can hardly jump or run. Therefore, our individual strength is firmly rooted in our collectives. Without those collectives, we would have no belonging, care, esteem, family, friends, love, power, safety, status, etc. We would have no buildings, computers, education, entertainment, equipment, information, insurance, healthcare, housing, infrastructure, internet, libraries, protection, satellites, science, space exploration, submarines, technology, telecommunication, etc. Certainly, we would have no credit cards! Even our cash depends on the collective. Money is the collective way to preserve a claim on resources over time. It has to be accepted by the members of the collective in order to remain valuable. None of those collective advantages could be created or maintained by unorganized individuals. A collective provides those advantages in exchange for individual freedom. With the individual acceptance of collective rights comes the responsibility of that individual to accept the collective obligations. As Confucius said—*Do not do to others what you do not want them to do to you.*

Any threat to your collectives is a direct threat to you. Therefore, maximizing the success of your collectives will maximize your own success. From that point of view, altruism, compassion, loyalty, morality, and philanthropy are personal necessities. It is in your interest to support your family, business, tribe, nation, and ultimately, the entire human race. Paradoxically, competent competitors will cooperate! You can only maximize your success by supporting others. Keep your collectives united and strong. Turn their weaknesses into strengths, and their threats into opportunities. Only incompetent people cut off the branch they are sitting on. For example, Marcus Brutus paid with his life for murdering his powerful benefactor and possible father Julius Caesar.

No matter how high you climb the mast of the Titanic, you go down when the ship goes down. Therefore, help yourself by helping others. Give them the chance to become the smartest thinkers they can be. Then, they can help you to find solutions. Support yourself by spreading nemonik thinking within your collectives.

Collectives try to give a higher natural authority to their rules by calling them laws. However, their rules remain arbitrary and, therefore, they have to be enforced by people. Without such enforcement, making artificial rules is unproductive. The individual advantages of offending without retribution could motivate people who normally obey the rules to become offenders. As economists say—*Bad money drives out good money.*[26] To prevent and suppress dissention, collectives are often forced to use aggression, authority, bureaucracy, coercion, control, dogmas, enforcement, escalation, judiciary, law and order, military, peer pressure, retribution, rules, secrets, suppression, verdicts, war, etc. On the other hand, strict enforcement of the rules fosters resentment, rebellion, and stagnation. Hence, rules are simultaneously a collective necessity and the seed of its destruction.

If the competent provide no leadership, then they will be ruled by the incompetent. As history shows, extreme imbalances in the distribution of wealth, status, privilege, and power lead ultimately to rebellion and violent social struggles. When this happens, the wealthy and powerful usually call for *justice* in order to protect the imbalances that support them. Their kind of justice results in maintaining the status quo by increasing law and order. Under the pretence of stabilising society, they act to defend the social inequalities and maintain their advantageous positions by calling for more justice. If their justice fails, then they will resort to aggression. As Lao Zi points out—*Superior propriety acts and if there is no reaction, the arms are bared and force will be used.*[27]

To curb an increasing disregard for the law, leaders will need increasingly more control in their attempts to maintain law and order—*When the people are not afraid of authority then greater authority will arise (Lao Zi).*[28] However, if a government becomes so controlling that it does not allow people to follow their natural inclination, then the people will become poor—*If the government is very strict, then the people will have extreme shortages (Lao Zi).*[29] If the collective becomes poor, then the leaders might fall and the collective might be taken over by another collective.

Before the French Revolution, the aristocracy in that country controlled the people with violence. The privileged maintained an artificial imbalance in wealth and freedom at the cost of the common people. The aristocracy was living for the sake of its own interest and ignored Lao Zi's *Dao* or *Way.*[30] The Way is the natural force that restores always the natural balance of reality. That correcting force manifested itself in the violence and aggression of the French revolution, which resulted in the storming of the hated Bastille in 1789. This popular uprising initiated the *Reign of Terror.* The violence unleashed to restore the balance was the result of the violence applied to maintain the imbalance.

Many great collectives have failed because the required rules have the tendency to become static in a dynamic reality. In order to create and maintain the artificial reality, believers in the collective doctrine have no choice but to inhibit change. Consequently, the natural dynamism of reality forces them to resort ultimately to extremism and brute force. This suppressive aggression is a sure path to disaster, because the use of force fosters an opposing force of equal strength. As Lao Zi points out—*The more law and order is developed, the more burglars and thieves there will be.*[31]

A collective could foster unintentionally mediocrity by providing a hiding place for incompetent people. Advocates of the collective might coerce individuals to support the team with the admonition—*There is no 'I' in team.* They blame the individual for not being a team player. However, their rhetoric ignores the fact that there are two *'I's* in winning. Although nemonik thinkers try to avoid conflict, they are sometimes forced to compete. Many important things are based on competition—even finding that special person to share your life. However, be careful that competition does not distract you from maximizing the probability of success. Some people win every competition, but are never successful.

Sometimes, collective is the best solution to obtain what you seek and escape what you suffer. In other situations, the individual approach might be more effective. As with all nemonik thinking, the choice depends entirely on the situation. It is difficult to imagine that the ideas of scientists such as Nicolaus Copernicus, Sir Isaac Newton, or Albert Einstein could have been generated by a collective. No collective could have created theories about the orbit of the planet, gravity, or relativity. Neither could a collective have painted Leonardo da Vinci's *Mona Lisa.*[32]

Despite all the advantages of a collective, individualism is sometimes the better choice. Above all, it is in your interest to maximize your personal success. Therefore, act as a team member to make your collective succeed, but act as an individual to succeed within your collective.

Sir Richard's collective mindmode

Sir Richard's intentions to avoid court actions could suggest a mental bias against collective thinking .[33] However, some of his comments suggest otherwise. For instance, he maintains that there should be ethical standards concerning the treatment of customers, employees, suppliers, investors, and competitors. He also points out that the rules should apply equally to all stakeholders and that one should know when and how to negotiate contracts.[34] Furthermore, he is likely to have applied collective thinking in his conflict with British Airways. That case involved collectives such as the CAA, European Commission, Japanese Intergovernmental Agreement, Monopolies and Mergers Commission, Traffic Distribution Rules, and Heathrow Slot Committee.[35] Furthermore, his comments suggest that he supports his collectives because he is passionate about his family, friends, companies, charities, and peace activities.[36]

Notes

AFFECTORIAL NEMONIKS

Table 05 illustrates that the two exhaustive parts of affectorial thinking are the *creative and reactive* mindmodes.

Table 05: Affectorial nemoniks

- Nemonik thinking
  - Mind
    - Conscious
      - Rational thinking
        - OBJECTIVE-1
        - COLLECTIVE-2
    - Subconscious
      - Affectorial thinking
        - **CREATIVE-3**
        - **REACTIVE-4**
  - Reality
    - Space
      - ADVANCE-5
      - STAY-6
      - RETREAT-7
    - Matter
      - ACCUMULATE-8
      - PRESERVE-9
      - DISPOSE-10
    - Time
      - ACT-11
      - WAIT-12
      - PREPARE-13
  - Interaction
    - Perception
      - ACCEPT-14
      - REJECT-15
    - Projection
      - REVEAL-16
      - CONCEAL-17

AFFECTORIAL NEMONIK 3—CREATIVE

The creative mindmode is a way of affectorial thinking that deals with the chaos of reality by generating creative affecters. Creative affecters are new descriptions of the chaos of reality, which are generated by the creative mindmode. They include discoveries, fantasies, ideas, innovations, insights, inspirations, inventions, novelties, etc. The creative mindmode provides new experiences and, therefore, it moves you outside your comfort zone. However, creativity is sometimes unrealistic.

Keywords for *creative* include: *art, brainstorm, conception, creative affecters, creativity, different, discoveries, disorganizing, divergent thinking, exceptional, fantasy, hatching, ideas, incubation, inexperience, innovations, insights, inspirations, inventions, lateral thinking, new, novel, original, progress, questions, randomizing, unknown, etc.*[37]

The literature of behavioural psychology contains many reports of subjects responding randomly after the experimenter withholds the reinforcements for previously reinforced behaviour. When facing such chaos, the subjects seem to apply the strategy of random *Try and error.*[38] Furthermore, brainstorming is a non-critical group technique that creates randomly ideas by fostering a silent mind, free expression, and association, while inhibiting rational thinking.

The processes underlying the creative mindmode cannot be observed directly because they are hidden in the subconscious. Nevertheless, the previous observations support the notion that the creative mindmode disorganizes or randomizes available information until it finds a *Best Fit* for the actual situation. Like a fruit machine, if the result lines up with reality, then you hit the jackpot. The creative mindmode has to unfreeze Spencer's *known* by disorganization. Otherwise, the mind remains stuck in the reactive groove of memory. In that case, it could only recall information without originality. Hence, the *unknown* of the mental chaos generated by the creative mindmode deals with the *unknown* chaos of reality.

Mental disorganization of the *known* is a non-rational way of exploring the *unknown.* As a result, creative affecters might not stand up to rational scrutiny. Nevertheless, creative thinking is needed, because rational thinking cannot deal with the chaos of reality. Rational thinking requires order, predictability, laws, rules, and facts, which are by definition unavailable in the chaos of reality. Therefore, the non-rationality of the creative mindmode is a strength, rather than a weakness. Furthermore, the seventeen nemoniks are memory prompts and markers for mind mapping that foster the associative processes of the creative mindmode. A mind map is a diagram showing the relationship between concepts. Stay with me—it is all about you!

Joy Paul Guilford (1897-1987) was a US psychologist who introduced the concepts of convergent and divergent thinking. Convergent thinking is a way of thinking that aims to provide the only correct answer on a specific question. Divergent thinking is a creative way of thinking that aims to provide multiple solutions for a single problem.

Edward de Bono (1933--) is a Maltese consultant, inventor, and physician who introduced lateral thinking in 1970. Lateral thinking is a creative way of thinking that reformulates problems and looks at them from different perspectives in order to find solutions.[39] Lateral thinking was de Bono's reaction to the 'vertical way' of thinking proposed by the 'gang of three', which comprises the philosophers Socrates, Plato, and Aristotle from ancient Greece. Although very popular, lateral thinking is not a complete way thinking and cannot replace rational thinking.

An important part of problem solving is identifying the right problems. After all, correct solutions for unproductive problems are still unproductive solutions. Divergent and lateral thinking are both too much solution oriented without sufficiently addressing adequately the evaluation of the specific problem. In contrast, the exhaustive nemonik template prompts all mindmodes to reveal and reformulate all problems by generating questions and ideas from each possible perspective. The nemonik template is a generator of questions and ideas, which adds procedure and structure to creative thinking. Nemonik thinking is lateral thinking on steroids.

Solution oriented thinking could be a threat. Unproductive questions produce unproductive answers. Consider the question (2 x 8 = ?). A rational thinker is likely to apply the tables of multiplication and replies 16. However, that answer assumes limitations because the question was to provide something that is equal to 2 x 8. It did not ask for a number. Therefore, a creative thinker would be free to include arithmetic operations in the answer such as adding, subtracting, multiplication, division, raising the power, and drawing the square root. As a result, the answer becomes an infinite string of equal values. For example, $2 \times 8 = 16 = 11 + 5 = 20 - 4 = 2 \times 2 \times 4 = 32 / 2 = 4^2 = \sqrt{256}$ etc. Each answer is correct, but also meaningless without defining the question more precisely. Such as, express the multiplication as a number, addition, subtraction, multiplication, division, power, or square root. This shows that a rational thinker is likely to follow the collective rules. In contrast, it is the essence of creative thinkers to avoid such conventions. Creative thinkers are likely to generate questions that challenge rational thinkers. Hence, creative thinking should provide the right questions before rational thinking could provide the right answers.

Sir Richard's creative mindmode

Sir Richard adheres to a philosophy of ongoing creativity for himself, his team, and his business. He mentions that his imagination expands beyond what he reads and that his ideas often come from nowhere. Ideas are precious and, therefore, he uses notebooks to capture each idea that he generates and encounters.[40]

Difficulties seem to inspire him. When his holiday flight from Beef Island was cancelled, he started Virgin Airways to get home. In addition, he told Nik Powell that some people at Student Magazine were unhappy with Nik's ideas. Sir

Richard created that story on the spot to counteract Nik's attempt to remove him as publisher and editor of the magazine.[41]

Sir Richard also incorporates external creativity such as Randolph Fields' idea for an Atlantic airline, Patrick Zelnick's proposal for the Paris Megastore, Toby Helm's inquiry about the operation of British trains, Gerry Spencer's suggestion for Virgin Cola, and Rowan Gormley's introduction to financial-services. Daring ideas have been a driving force behind Virgin's expansion. However, Sir Richard mentions that the summit of this creative development was the quantum leap from Virgin Records to Virgin Atlantic.[42]

AFFECTORIAL NEMONIK 4—REACTIVE

The reactive mindmode is a way of affectorial thinking that deals with the chaos of reality by habituating mindsets that generate reactive affecters. Reactive refers to a mental or physical response without conscious thinking that is initiated by the reactive mindmode. Habituation is a mental process that derives mindsets from repetitive actions and thoughts.

Mindsets are internalized sets of rules that are derived by the reactive mindmode from the past, the known, or experience in order to generate reactive affecters. Mindsets increase the speed and accuracy of a person's mental and physical actions. Every repeated behaviour or thought becomes ultimately a mindset. In computer terminology, mindsets could be compared to algorithms. An algorithm is a set of rules comprising a computational procedure, which follows a definite path to the single solution of a problem.

Reactive affecters are generated by mindsets and deal with the chaos of reality. They include anger, beliefs, common sense, desires, emotions, feelings, habits, hate, heuristics, impulses, intuitions, love, reactions, reflexes, routines, sensibilities, skills, etc. It is the aim of the reactive mindmode to optimize one's mental and physical perfection.

Keywords for *reactive* include: *accurate, belief, common sense, confidence, desires, efficient, emergency, emotions, sensibility, experience, faith, feelings, gut-feeling, habituation, hate, heuristics, hunch, impulses, individual perfection, informal logic, love, instinct, intuition, mindsets, motivation, order, passion, predictable, rash, reactions, reactive affecters, reflexes, routines, skills, speed, stability, traits, etc.*

The reactive mindmode prepares mental order to deal with the chaos of reality. For example, the time and severity of floods are unknown, because they are associated with the chaos of reality. However, the reactive mindmode could prepare a mindset for swimming. In that case, the response to any unpredictable flood becomes predictable. You just move your arms and legs in the internalized way and you will survive. Hence, the reactive mindmode prepares predictable order to deal with the unpredictable chaos of reality. Reactive thinking relies on your experience and, therefore, it keeps you within your comfort zone and fosters stagnation. Hence, reactive thinking is associated with Spencer's *known*.

The reactive mindmode fosters personal perfection by maximizing individual performance through successive approximation. It is like aiming a bow and arrow. During the first attempt, you might aim too low and the arrow hit the ground. During the second attempt, you might aim too high so that your arrow overshoots the target. The third time, you adjust your aim again and so on until you hit the target. You learn from your mistakes and move on! It is a process of trying, failing, and adjusting until you reach success. Each time you perform a task, your reactive mindmode hones the particular mindset closer towards perfection. After each improvement, the mindset requires less conscious attention and, therefore, it sinks deeper into the subconscious. Ultimately, you can execute the task automatically with a silent mind.

Another example of developing a mindset is learning how to drive a car. Initially, you have no mindset and have to think consciously about each action. With the improvement of your mindset, the need for conscious control decreases and the mindset sinks deeper into your subconscious. Ultimately, your subconscious activates the mindset for driving and hits the brakes before your conscious even realizes the danger.

The reactive mindmode has also been the basis for the development of Eastern martial arts such as karate and taekwondo. A competent warrior fights with a silent mind—if you have to think consciously about your next move then you are too slow. You would be dead. As long as you are thinking consciously about the execution of your actions, then you are still learning. If that case, your conscious is still interfering with the affecters and you will need more exercise.

The subconscious works on a need-to-know basis. It does not release the reasons behind the affecters that it sends to the conscious. If the subconscious mindset is perfect then the conscious does not need to know anything because the reactive mindmode will execute the action. This need-to-know basis is perfect for physical and mental emergencies because there is no time for learning or contemplating. If you fall in a roaring river, then it is too late to read a book about survival in the wilderness. Your reactive mindmode has to activate your mindset for swimming and if you have polished that mindset enough then you might survive. That mindset might not comprise perfect swimming skills, but it contains the best skill that you have available at that time.

Informal logic is the part of reason that might be based on former formal logic that the reactive mindmode has transformed into mindsets. Those mindsets influence the conscious with affecters such as aphorisms. The advantage is that informal logic is efficient and provides instantaneously a *Best Fit* for the actual situation. For example, we might conclude immediately that the previously mentioned elephant is larger than the mouse, without applying formal logic.

The advantage of informal logic is simplicity and speed, which comes often at the cost of an imperfect fit to reality. Furthermore, it is impossible to explain the evidence underlying informal logic to others because those explanations are hidden in the subconscious. For those reasons, rationalization is often used to transform informal logic back into explainable formal logic. During a rationalization, people accept the conclusion before they create a pseudo-rational argument to support that conclusion. Some people present their informal logic incorrectly as formal logic in order to gain the natural authority of formal logic.

Intuitions are reactive affecters that are created from information stored in the subconscious in order to protect the conscious from information overload. Some suggest that we should follow our intuition. However, the subconscious creates a seamless reality and hides information from the conscious. We have no conscious information about the subconscious reasons underlying our intuitions. Hence, the feeling that we can trust our intuition might be just a false sense of security.

Each day, there are millions of transactions on the global share markets. Each transaction is an agreement between a seller and a buyer and, therefore, the number of buyers and sellers is the same. All those traders rely mainly on their intuition because trading based on inside information is illegal. Nevertheless, half the traders follow their intuition to sell, while the other half follow their intuition to buy. One-half of the traders expect an increase in a particular fund, while the other half expects a decrease in the same fund. Consequently, half of those intuitions are wrong, supporting the notion that intuitions about the share market are unreliable. Nevertheless, the belief of the winning traders in their intuition will be reinforced.

The first impression is crucial. Most people have experienced an immediate liking or disliking of a stranger. Often such intuitions are proven correct by the subsequent behaviour of that person. Although intuitions are important to make fast decisions about people, they are also self-fulfilling prophesies. If I were to act on a negative intuition about a stranger, then it is likely that my behaviour towards that person becomes negative. In that case, even the most positive person might act negatively in response to my negative behaviour. My expectations would be the cause of that negative feedback. Hence, we have to scrutinize our intuitions about people very carefully. As they say—*Do not judge a book by its cover.* This is not to say that intuition is trivial, but be aware of its weaknesses.

You can only trust your intuition if you have prepared it carefully. If you want to be ready for emergencies, then you have to prepare the appropriate mindsets in advance. If you want to respond intuitively as a Karate fighter, then you have to exercise your katas. If you want to be a smarter thinker, then it is in your interest to create a mindset for nemonik thinking through study and training.

We do what we are, while we are what we do. Our actions determine our mindsets through learning, while our mindsets determine our actions through affecters. What we do today determines who we will be tomorrow. On the other hand, who we are determines what we do today. One will affect the other in endless cycles of habituation. If you study nemonik thinking today, then the resulting mindset will make you a better thinker tomorrow.

Habituation fosters stability in your thinking. The same situation is likely to evoke the same affecters. Other people like that because you become predictable. The downside is that predictability is a strategic weakness. Furthermore, the habituation of the reactive mindmode fosters static thinking in a dynamic reality. If you have to adjust to a fast changing environment, then mindsets expire rapidly. Nevertheless, the subconscious will protect those mindsets because their creation has cost precious time and effort. This could cause an internal conflict between the conscious need to adjust to reality versus the subconscious desire to maintain the status quo. That could explain why many people avoid change and suffer from cognitive dissonance.

The conscious ponders, but the subconscious decides. After the subconscious has made a decision, it sends affecters to the conscious to enforce that decision. However, in many cases, the subconscious has not decided yet. Therefore, the conscious does not know what to do, which fosters confusion. To examine consciously the subconscious information is by definition impossible. However, you could trick your reactive mindmode by enticing it to send an affecter. For that reason, you make a pseudo-decision by flipping a coin. The first feeling evoked by that fake decision might tell you what your subconscious thinks right now.

Sir Richard's reactive mindmode

Sir Richard's statements suggest that he relies on intuition and impulses, which allows him to make rapid decisions about people and issues. As a result, he is likely to prosper in chaos and to avoid the restraints of order and formality.[43] His reactive actions include his immediate response to rumours, closing down Event Magazine in order to cut his losses, offering The Rolling Stones and Janet Jackson immediately good deals, and his instant decision to operate trains.[44]

Risk-taking is as important as risk-avoidance for maximizing one's success. However, even the strongest intuition could be incorrect and might need a reality-check. Although Sir Richard has been very successful, the reversal of Virgin's flotation, the unforeseen collapse of MCEG, and the failure of the mini CD factory suggest that his reality-check on reactive thinking is not entirely flawless.[45] In his defence, Sir Richard points out that making mistakes is essential to learning and success.[46] Furthermore, Lao Zi points out—*Sages regard a weakness as a weakness; thus, it is not a weakness.*[47] In accord, Sir Richard recognizes his weaknesses and employs others to compensate for them.[48]

It is the prime aim of reactive thinking to foster one's physical and mental perfection through habituation. Therefore, reactive affecters are likely to become increasingly stable over time. As a result, reactive specialists tend to respond in the same way to similar conditions. In accord, Sir Richard seems to react consistently with determination, competition, and sensitivity to challenges.[49] On the other hand, Sir Richard warns that habituation could foster stagnation, which is a threat in our dynamic reality.[50]

<table>
<tr><td colspan="4">Table 06: Nemonik model of the mind</td></tr>
<tr><td colspan="4" align="center">MIND</td></tr>
<tr><td colspan="4" align="center">Information Overload</td></tr>
<tr><td colspan="2" align="center">relevant to the present</td><td colspan="2" align="center">irrelevant to the present</td></tr>
<tr><td colspan="2" align="center">Zen[51]
Conscious</td><td colspan="2" align="center">Freud[52]
Subconscious</td></tr>
<tr><td colspan="2" align="center">Aristotle[53]
Rational thinking</td><td colspan="2" align="center">Lao Zi[54]
Affectorial thinking</td></tr>
<tr><td colspan="2" rowspan="2" align="center">Lao Zi[55]</td><td colspan="2" align="center">Spencer[56]</td></tr>
<tr><td align="center">unknown</td><td align="center">known</td></tr>
<tr><td align="center">natural</td><td align="center">artificial</td><td align="center">future</td><td align="center">past</td></tr>
<tr><td align="center">Newton[57]
OBJECTIVE</td><td align="center">Confucius[58]
COLLECTIVE</td><td align="center">de Bono[59]
CREATIVE</td><td align="center">Lao Zi[60]
REACTIVE</td></tr>
</table>

Table 06 shows earlier contributions to the nemonik model of the mind. Each mindmode comprises a different interaction between the order or chaos of the mental process versus the order or chaos of reality. (1) The objective mindmode creates mental order to deal with the natural order of reality. (2) The collective mindmode creates mental order to deal with the artificial order of reality. (3) The creative mindmode creates mental chaos to deal with the chaos of reality. (4) The reactive mindmode creates mental order to deal with the chaos of reality.

There is a subtle difference between the objective and creative mindmodes. Objective specialists discover things that have been there all the time—there was always gravity in nature. On the other hand, creative specialists invent new things—the light bulb did not exist in nature. Furthermore, the difference between the creative and reactive mindmodes is illustrated in making music. Composing music and writing lyrics requires the creative mindmode, while playing and singing that same music involves the reactive mindmode. The first activity requires imagination, while the second one requires skill. Hence, not every musician has to be creative.

Some mindmodes use the same method to foster different goals. The objective and collective mindmodes both use rational thinking to obtain, respectively, natural facts and artificial ones. On the other hand, some mindmodes use different methods to foster the same goal. For example, the objective and creative mindmodes use, respectively, logic and imagination to foster progress.

Despite their differences, each of the four mindmodes has ultimately the same goal to maximize your success. Any long-term bias towards or against a mindmode is counterproductive because it fosters static thinking in a dynamic reality. Reality is always changing and, therefore, each mindmode is equally important. The value of each mindmode depends exclusively on the particular situation.

Table 07 shows the main characteristics associated with the four mindmodes.

Table 07: Characteristics of the mindmodes			
OBJECTIVE	COLLECTIVE	CREATIVE	REACTIVE
Conscious	Conscious	Subconscious	Subconscious
Rational	Rational	Affectorial	Affectorial
Natural	Artificial	Future	Past
order	order	chaos	chaos
predictable	predictable	unpredictable	predictable
reason	reason	silent mind	silent mind
fact	fact	affecter	affecter
concentrate	concentrate	meditate	meditate
distrust	distrust	trust	trust
dispassion	dispassion	passion	passion
organize	organize	disorganize	organize
causation	causation	inspiration	habituation
logic	logic	imagination	intuition
analyse	analyse	innovate	impulse
objective	collective	subjective	subjective
progress	perfection	progress	perfection
freedom	control	freedom	control
laws	rules	exceptions	skills
truth	verdict	idea	belief
test	negotiate	sleep	exercise
confirm	conform	associate	learn

REALITY

Everyone seems to have a fair idea about the essence of reality. After all, we have lived in it our entire life. Nevertheless, disagreements suggest that the perceived reality is difficult to describe. On close inspection, it seems to be a fluctuating collection of fuzzy material and mental components. Furthermore, descriptions of reality could be objective, collective, or subjective. Objective refers to a description of reality that is independent of what anyone believes. In contrast, collective descriptions depend on the beliefs of a particular group of people, while subjective descriptions depend on the beliefs of a particular individual. Hence, any description of reality is likely to be confounded by the source of that description. Nevertheless, we need a basic description of reality in order to discuss nemonik thinking.

Table 08: The structure of reality.

External Reality		
Sensory	Extrasensory	
	Scientific	Supernatural
known	unknown	unknowable[61]
Internal Reality		

Table 08 shows the structure of reality. The external reality comprises material and immaterial phenomena that surround the mind. The sensory reality is that part of the external reality that can be examined directly through the natural human senses. The extrasensory reality is the part of the external reality that cannot be perceived through the natural human senses such as microorganisms and black holes. The extrasensory reality comprises the scientific and supernatural realities. The scientific reality is the part of the extrasensory reality that can be perceived with artificial sensors or rational thinking such as infrared light. The supernatural reality is the part of the extrasensory reality that is outside the scientific reality. It includes such phenomena as clairvoyance, divine power, ESP, extrasensory perception, God, paranormal, precognition, PSI, psychokinesis, spirit, telekinesis, and telepathy. The internal reality is the subjective spatial, material, and temporal conscious perception of the external reality that is created by the subconscious. That is what you perceive as reality. Spatial refers to space, material to matter, and temporal to time.

If not otherwise indicated, reality refers in this book to the sensory reality. Senses are integrated physiological and mental systems that perceive material signals from the sensory reality and transform them into neural signals. The five traditional senses are hearing, seeing, smelling, tasting, and touching. However, we also sense balance, body position, movement, pain, pressure, temperature, etc. At this stage, those simple definitions are sufficient for nemonik thinking. The essence of reality will be discussed elsewhere.[62]

Albert Einstein (1879-1955) was a Swiss scientist who published in 1905 three papers that revolutionized Newtonian physics. In addition, Einstein's former tutor, Hermann Minkowski, proposed that reality comprises a space-time continuum.[63] However, that is not the way our mind perceives daily reality. In our mind, space and time are separate phenomena. Furthermore, Michio Kaku reported in his book *Hyperspace* that some mathematical formulas describing reality require either 10 or 26 dimensions in order to remain self-consistent.[64] Nevertheless, simple observation suggests that we are physically excluded from those hyper-dimensions. It is like being confined to 4 rooms of a mansion that contains either 6 or 22 hidden rooms. Hence, our mental processes can only be based on the illusionary four separate dimensions of space and time that most people seem to perceive.

Spencer emphasized the concepts of the *known, unknown, and unknowable.* Although natural laws and artificial rules provide predictability, we have to know them before we can take advantage of that predictability. If we do not know the natural laws, then we might still plant our seeds at the wrong time of the year and starve. If we do not know the artificial rules, then we might get killed by driving on the wrong side of the road. Affectorial thinking deals with the chaos of reality by taking into account Spencer's concepts of both the *known* and *unknown*. In accord, the creative mindmode deals with the *unknown* future, while the reactive mindmode relies on the *known* past. Furthermore, Spencer's concept of the *unknowable* underlies many religious conflicts concerning interpretations and efforts to turn the *unknowable* into the *known*. Although interesting, the *unknowable* or supernatural is outside the scope of nemonik thinking.

Your internal reality is affected by your attitudes, beliefs, emotions, expectations, experiences, knowledge, memories, morals, sensory perceptions, thoughts, etc. Therefore, the internal reality of each person is different. The same external reality could be one person's internal heaven and another person's internal hell. Consequently, a person's behaviour can only be understood within the context of that person's internal reality.

Notes

PARTS OF THE SENSORY REALITY

Table 09 illustrates that the three exhaustive parts of the sensory reality are space, matter, and time. They are the external resources to maximize your success. Nemonik thinkers aim to turn spatial, material and temporal weaknesses into strengths, and threats into opportunities.

Table 09: Parts of the sensory reality				
Nemonik thinking				
	Mind			
		Conscious		
			Rational thinking	
				OBJECTIVE-1
				COLLECTIVE-2
		Subconscious		
			Affectorial thinking	
				CREATIVE-3
				REACTIVE-4
	Reality			
			Space	
				ADVANCE-5
				STAY-6
				RETREAT-7
			Matter	
				ACCUMULATE-8
				PRESERVE-9
				DISPOSE-10
			Time	
				ACT-11
				WAIT-12
				PREPARE-13
	Interaction			
			Perception	
				ACCEPT-14
				REJECT-15
			Projection	
				REVEAL-16
				CONCEAL-17

Space

Space is the three-dimensional, infinite, and nonmaterial part of reality in which matter is immersed and moves around. The three spatial dimensions are latitude, longitude, and altitude. Space can be perceived indirectly by evaluating the size of material objects and the distance between them. Too much space weakens your supply lines and is hard to control. Too little space restricts your movements and leaves too much space for your opponents to outmanoeuvre you. Hence, if you want to maximize your success, then it is in your interest to manage space carefully. Space is managed by applying the exhaustive nemoniks to *advance, stay, and retreat.*

Matter

Matter is the three-dimensional finite part of reality that features substance, volume, and weight, and occupies and moves through space and time. Similar to the spatial dimensions, the three dimensions of material volume are width, depth, and height. Matter is the part of sensory reality that you can perceive directly with your senses.

Matter can be transformed and moved in order to maximize your success. It can be organic such as living animals, plants and people, or inorganic, such as lifeless iron, rock and water. Hence, matter includes resources such as animals, energy, equipment, information, money, people, plants, raw materials, etc. Information is classified as matter because it cannot exist without matter. Even mentally, we can only store information by changing the matter that constitutes our brains. Furthermore, energy is just another manifestation of matter, as shown by Einstein's formula $E = mc^2$.

The presence of matter can be dangerous. Julius Caesar was stabbed to death in the presence of Marcus Brutus and the Roman Senators. The presence of water might flood your house, while the presence of a concrete pole could suddenly stop your car. You could also be in the presence of a case filled with dynamite. On the other hand, the absence of matter can be as dangerous as its presence. Think about the absence of air, food, money, shelter, and water! Shakespeare was well aware of the dangers involved in the absence of matter when he had King Richard III proclaim—*My kingdom for a horse.*[65] In that play, the absence of a horse cost dear Richard his life. In the same way, the absence of his Praetorian Guard was fatal for Julius Caesar. Insufficient matter fosters deprivation.

The presence and absence of matter can be either advantageous or dangerous. Therefore, it is to your advantage to manage matter carefully. Matter is managed by applying the exhaustive nemoniks to *accumulate, preserve, and dispose.*

Time

Time is the one-dimensional, eternal, and nonmaterial part of reality that can be perceived indirectly by changes in matter and the movement of matter through space.

Given enough time, we can replace, repair, and learn to live with almost anything. Hence, make haste slowly and do not give up hope. Time is also a great equalizer because it is scarce for everyone. Independent of the amount of space and matter that we have to our disposal, each of us has exactly 24 hours in a day. You could hire others to do some work for you, but your own time is irreplaceable. Every second gone is gone forever. Therefore, time is a precious commodity. The clock keeps ticking—live each day as if it is the last one!

Insufficient time fosters panic. If you want to maximize your success, then it is in your interest to manage your time very carefully. Time is managed by applying the exhaustive nemoniks to *act, wait, and prepare.*

SPATIAL NEMONIKS

Table 10 illustrates that the three exhaustive spatial nemoniks are *advance, stay, and retreat.* Any detour extends the distance to your goal and, therefore, it is a retreat, rather than a separate spatial nemonik.

Table 10: Spatial nemoniks

- Nemonik thinking
  - Mind
    - Conscious
      - Rational thinking
        - OBJECTIVE-1
        - COLLECTIVE-2
    - Subconscious
      - Affectorial thinking
        - CREATIVE-3
        - REACTIVE-4
  - Reality
    - Space
      - **ADVANCE-5**
      - **STAY-6**
      - **RETREAT-7**
    - Matter
      - ACCUMULATE-8
      - PRESERVE-9
      - DISPOSE-10
    - Time
      - ACT-11
      - WAIT-12
      - PREPARE-13
  - Interaction
    - Perception
      - ACCEPT-14
      - REJECT-15
    - Projection
      - REVEAL-16
      - CONCEAL-17

SPATIAL NEMONIK 5—ADVANCE

Advance is the spatial nemonik that prompts the mind to decrease the distance to a goal. A goal is an intended individual or collective achievement, which could be either a mission or a target. A mission is a long-term or ultimate goal of a person or collective. A target is a short-term goal that could be a step towards the completion of a mission.

Keywords for *advance* include: *assault, attack, challenge, charge, chase, conquer, develop, enter, expand, explore, forward, infiltrate, invade, move ahead, offensive, overrun, penetrate, progress, proliferate, promote, pursue, push, seize, storm, strike, etc.*

My mission is to help people to become the smartest thinkers they can be. Finishing this book is my current target in the completion of that mission. If you want to maximize your success, then it is in your interest to select a direction in life. Otherwise, you might go around in circles. Advancing gives you the initiative to decide when, where, and how to operate. However, in chaotic times it might be counterproductive to pursue your goal. Such a fixed direction would reduce your ability to take advantage of the opportunities created by the dynamism of reality. Again, whether to advance or not depends on the actual situation.

Between the First and Second World War, the German Panzer commander General Heinz Wilhelm Guderian (1888-1954) introduced the concept of *Blitzkrieg*. Blitzkrieg is a coordinated high-speed advance that features momentum, mutual assistance between units, bypassing obstacles, and concentration on the ultimate goal. Fast moving tanks were the core, while infantry, artillery, and air force provided support. The specific strengths of each unit covered the inherent weaknesses of the other ones. The speed of electronic communications and forward command enabled Guderian to integrate all units into a single coherent force. Blitzkrieg was the integration of industrial and military potential that outclassed traditional warfare. It proved to be very successful.

In 1940, Germany defeated, within six weeks, the allied forces of France, Britain, and the Low Countries. Beyond the destructive setting of war, the principles underlying a Blitzkrieg-type advance apply to many facets of daily life.

An advance might lead you into the dangers of unknown territory and overextended supply lines. Although *advance* had been initially the superior nemonik for the Germans, the situation changed dramatically when they decided to invade the Soviet Union. On 22 June 1941, about 3,600,000 soldiers, 3,600 tanks, and 2,700 aircrafts invaded the Soviet Union along a front of 2,000 miles reaching from the Baltic Sea to the Black Sea.[66] Codenamed Barbarossa, it was the largest military campaign ever commenced. For their defence, the Russians used a scorched earth strategy in an already naturally hostile climate. Scorched earth is a military strategy to destroy everything during a retreat, so that the invader cannot use those resources.

During Barbarossa, the Germans operated simultaneously on many widely separated fronts, stretching their resources beyond their limits. The long distance to Moscow overextended and exposed their supply lines. To add to the confusion on the Eastern front, the German high-command interrupted the advance and ignored protests from field commanders such as Guderian. The campaign changed from blitzkrieg into protracted warfare.

Advancing to a position you cannot defend is counterproductive. Without gain, you waste precious resources in the advance and the subsequent retreat. With the invasion of Russia, the scale of the war increased dramatically and the previously productive nemonik to *advance* became counterproductive. As a result, the German campaign became a total disaster and ended in a rout.

Sir Richard and advancing

Sir Richard mentions that he prefers to advance. This is evident from the expansion of Student Magazine into a massive global enterprise ranging from cosmetics to airlines. His preference for taking the initiative is shown in stalking EMI for a takeover, his quick bids for Janet Jackson and The Rolling Stones, and the immediate suppression of rumours.[67] Furthermore, he maintains a forceful momentum during his advance with a strong competitive attitude and determination. This is evident in setting up the mail-order business to save Student Magazine, opening retail shops to save the mail-order business, ignoring his financial problems with Nova Scotia to sign up Janet Jackson, and ignoring his problems with British Airways to sign up The Rolling Stones.[68] Despite his preference to advance, Sir Richard avoids personal confrontations. Therefore, he bypassed people such as Nik Powell, Don Cruickshank, his entire board, and the London branch of the Nova Scotia Bank.[69] Sir Richard's business strategy shows similarities to Guderian's blitzkrieg. Fast and focussed! If you cannot get through a concrete wall, then get around it, but keep advancing.

SPATIAL NEMONIK 6—STAY

Stay is the spatial nemonik that prompts the mind to maintain the same distance to the goal.

Keywords for *stay* include: *broken down, defend, entrench, freeze, halt, idle, immobile, immovable, inactive, inert, inflexible, inoperative, motionless, paralysed, passive, restrain, rigid, stable, stagnate, stall, standby, static, stationary, still, stop, unmoving, etc.*

Although staying might not bring you any closer to your target, it could be an effective defence against superior forces if you hold a strong position. Furthermore, staying provides the opportunity to consolidate your progress. Consolidating your gains could prevent you from losing everything during your next advance. Threats associated with staying are the loss of initiative, momentum, and direction. A strong fort could become a strong trap.

Sun Zi suggests—*Competent generals do not fight.*[70] Competent generals outmanoeuvre their opponents. In that way, they accumulate undamaged resources, while preserving their own. Otherwise, a third party might take the spoils of your efforts. After the Second World War, Germany became Europe's economic powerhouse by staying within its borders. What would have happened in 1940 if the Germans had chosen to stay, rather than advance?

Sir Richard and staying

Sir Richard's successful advance might have fostered some of the consolidation problems, which were manifest in Virgin's overdrafts with Coutts Bank, Nova Scotia Bank, and Lloyds Bank.[71] Insufficient funds caused high-risk situations that threatened the long-term success of the Virgin Group. In army terminology, the supply-lines carrying money became overextended. However, Sir Richard's comments suggest that he knowingly accepted those risks. He chose to maintain the momentum of his advance, rather than playing it safe by staying and consolidating his gains. The success of the Virgin

Group supports the notion that his intuition to maintain his momentum was correct.

SPATIAL NEMONIK 7—RETREAT

Retreat is the spatial nemonik that prompts the mind to increase the distance to the goal.

Keywords for *retreat* include: *abandon, apologize, backward, concede, constrict, defeated, depart, desert, disengage, dissociate, divorce, escape, evacuate, exit, exodus, fall back, flight, leave, pull back, recede, recoil, regress, resign, retire, retract, return, reverse, rout, setback, shrink, stampede, turn around, vacate, withdraw, etc.*

The ego is not a good strategist. If you want to maximize your success, then it is not in your interest to let your pride prevent a necessary retreat. Know when to cut your losses! Retreat to fight another day. A strategic retreat might increase your strength by leading you back into known territory and shortening your supply lines. It could also provide an opportunity to regroup your resources or to lure your opponents into an ambush.

Retreat carries the seed of defeat. Retreating to a position without an exit is a threat. Another danger of retreating is the possibility that it gains uncontrolled momentum. In that way, a strategic retreat could become a chaotic rout. A retreat might also create a power-vacuum that attracts opportunists or motivates your opponents to advance. As I mentioned previously, every decision depends on the actual situation.

Sir Richard and retreating

There is no gain without pain and Sir Richard advanced sometimes to positions where he could not stay. Although he prefers to advance, he proved to be realistic enough to retreat if necessary. For instance, he cut his losses and closed down Event Magazine, reversed the flotation of the Virgin Group through a management buyout, aborted the attempt to buy EMI, and sold Virgin Music in order to save Virgin Atlantic.[72] The sale of Virgin Music could be seen as a strategic retreat because the Virgin Group survived to fight another day. Without losing his momentum, Sir Richard regrouped his enterprise and came back into the music industry with V2 Music.[73] This shows that a retreat can lead ultimately to victory.

Notes

MATERIAL NEMONIKS

Table 11 illustrates that the three exhaustive material nemoniks are *accumulate, preserve, and dispose.* Transformation is the simultaneous accumulation of one type of matter by disposing another type of matter. To accumulate steel, one has to dispose of ore and energy. Hence, transformation is a combination of nemoniks, rather than a separate one.

Kenny Rogers' song about an old gambler reflects on the wisdom of managing your resources. The gambler explains that you have to know when to hold your cards, when to fold them, when to walk away, and when to run. Can you figure out which material nemoniks are mentioned in the lyrics and which one is missing? Why would the strategies of an old gambler differ from the strategies needed to maximize your success? You will find my suggestion in the endnotes.[74]

Table 11: Material nemoniks

- Nemonik thinking
  - Mind
    - Conscious
      - Rational thinking
        - OBJECTIVE-1
        - COLLECTIVE-2
    - Subconscious
      - Affectorial thinking
        - CREATIVE-3
        - REACTIVE-4
  - Reality
    - Space
      - ADVANCE-5
      - STAY-6
      - RETREAT-7
    - Matter
      - **ACCUMULATE-8**
      - **PRESERVE-9**
      - **DISPOSE-10**
    - Time
      - ACT-11
      - WAIT-12
      - PREPARE-13
  - Interaction
    - Perception
      - ACCEPT-14
      - REJECT-15
    - Projection
      - REVEAL-16
      - CONCEAL-17

MATERIAL NEMONIK 8—ACCUMULATE

Accumulate is the material nemonik that prompts the mind to increase the amount of matter that is under control.

Keywords for *accumulate* include: *accrue, acquire, add, amalgamate, amass, annex, assemble, borrow, buy, collect, construct, cultivate, develop, earn, enlarge, forage, gain, greed, grow, hire, hoard, invest, manufacture, mine, obtain, own, possess, procure, produce, profit, purchase, raid, seize, steal, take, etc.*

Accumulation could move you away from the dangerous edge of survival. Julius Caesar could have saved his life by accumulating his Praetorian Guard on his way to the Roman Senate. On the other hand, accumulation of status brings its own dangers because lightning strikes usually at the highest place.

Greed is accumulation for the sake of accumulation. As they say—*Some know the price of everything and the value of nothing.* Greed causes material imbalances and, therefore, it is likely to evoke counterproductive collective friction. Greed could become a trap that drives people to waste their precious time by accumulating matter that they do not need to achieve their goals. Possessions can become a heavy burden that exhausts even the strongest person during the journey through life. Desires lure us to places of death. *A room filled with gold and jade cannot be defended (Lao Zi).*[75] Therefore, it is in your interest to accumulate only matter that will maximize your success.

Sir Richard and accumulating

Sir Richard's accumulation is based on a business philosophy that includes competition, home-grown companies, internal financing through reinvested revenues, and external financing through bank loans, flotations, and joint-ventures.[76]

Accumulating capable people is another important feature of Sir Richard's philosophy. He attracts them with an easy-going attitude characterized by avoiding personal conflicts, holding no grudges, and sharing his success.[77] Within his organisation, his employees are his first priority. Therefore, he selects the right people, delegates authority, holds them accountable, maintains personal contact, motivates them to improve, praises rather than criticizes, fosters promotions, gives second changes, and compensates for weaknesses by incorporating experts.[78] Outside his organisation, he provides his customers with a good deal, fosters supplier loyalty, and protects his investors.[79] Hence, his philosophy is based on reciprocity—care for others and they will care for you.

With this philosophy, Sir Richard accumulated a considerable amount of possessions since starting *Student Magazine*. His interests include airlines, airship advertising, brand-consultancy, communications, computer consumables, computer games, cosmetics, a film studio, financial services, a holiday provider, a mail-order company, megastores, Necker Island, nightclubs, a publishing house, railways, a record label, recording studios, retail shops, soft drinks, etc.[80]

MATERIAL NEMONIK 9—PRESERVE

Preserve is the material nemonik that prompts the mind to maintain the same amount of matter that is under control.

Keywords for *preserve* include: *care, conserve, consolidate, contain, custody, defend, depot, fortify, hold, keep, look after, maintain, protect, retain, reserve, safeguard, save, secure, shelter, spare, stock, store, sustain, tend, etc.*

An advantage of preservation is that it maintains a buffer against material misfortune. It provides resources during periods of need. Furthermore, preservation protects previous investments in the accumulated matter that is under your control. A threat is that preserved matter has the tendency to deteriorate, which in physics is called *entropy* or the *arrow of time.*[81]

Memorizing information is the mental equivalent of material preservation. Nevertheless, even information that is preserved perfectly has a tendency to become outdated. Our dynamic era is inundated with new ideas. It is a threat to waste precious time preserving things that cannot be preserved. Preservation of matter cost resources and, therefore, preservation destroys resources. Around the time of the Industrial Revolution, many aristocrats tried to preserve their huge estates until their efforts ruined them. Reality changes—know when to let go!

Sir Richard and preserving

People are the core of Sir Richard's business and, therefore, he goes to great length to preserve them.[82] Although he mentions that he preserves the cash-flow of his organization, some overextensions caused serious problems. During those meagre times, he tried desperately to preserve his employees. Sir Richard and his directors did not pay themselves and even sold their cars, before he reluctantly laid off some employees.[83] Sir Richard also preserved the loyalty of his supplying artists by fostering personal relationships between them and the members of his organisation.[84] Furthermore, he preserved the goodwill of investors by buying Virgin shares back at the flotation price, rather than taking advantage of the much lower market value.[85] On the down side, he preserved shares in MCEG and lost $83 million during the crash of that company.[86] Sir Richard warns that preservation can foster stagnation.

MATERIAL NEMONIK 10—DISPOSE

Dispose is the material nemonik that prompts the mind to decrease the amount of matter that is under control.

Keywords for *dispose* include: *abandon, abolish, alienate, assassinate, banish, breakup, cast off, delete, demolish, depose, destroy, detach, disband, discard, discharge, discriminate, dismiss, dispel, disregard, divorce, eject, eliminate, eradicate, erase, exile, expel, exterminate, extinguish, let go, move on, obsolete, ostracise, outdated, purge, reduce, redundant, remove, separate, split, squander, terminate, waste, etc.*

Julius Caesar could have saved his life by disposing Marcus Brutus and the Roman senators before those assassins could act. A weakness of disposing of matter is the loss of previous investments in the accumulation and preservation of that matter. Furthermore, what is disposed today might be needed tomorrow. After all, disposals are notoriously hard to undo. Therefore, frugal people warn—*Waste not, want not!* Nevertheless, valuable matter might have to be disposed in order to improve your mobility and safety. Hence—*Hang on tightly and let go lightly (Proverb).*

Material gifts decrease the amount of matter that is available to you. Therefore, gifts are classified as a disposal of matter. In addition, what you might consider a precious gift might not be appreciated by the receiver. Gold is considered a precious metal. Nevertheless, even a greedy person might select a cheap sip of water over gold if thirsty enough. Therefore, a great gift requires a careful study of the recipient. In addition, what people desire is not always what they need. Hence, a competent leader focuses on needs, rather than desires.

Sir Richard and disposing

Due to the growth of Virgin Mail Order, Sir Richard attempted to sell Student Magazine to IPC, while fierce competition forced him to cut his losses and dispose of Event Magazine. Furthermore, he disposed of the Sega licence and Virgin Vision. The most prominent disposal was the reluctant sale of Virgin Music to EMI in order to save Virgin Atlantic.[87] During financial hardship, Sir Richard initiated radical disposals involving real estate, retail stock, artists, and even the cars and payments to the directors including himself.[88]

On two occasions, Sir Richard was forced to dispose of employees and some of the supplying artists.[89] Apparently, the most personal disposal was that of his friend Nik Powell, who tried to remove him from Student Magazine. Nevertheless, Sir Richard invited Nik back to the Virgin Mail Order Records company. After that, the growing demands of the organisation seemed to have outgrown Nik's abilities and emphasized their personal differences. In the end, they made the wise decision to split-up before it ruined their friendship.[90] Furthermore, Sir Richard disposed of Randolph Fields because he was apparently not the right manager for Virgin Atlantic.[91] Hence, Sir Richard's disposals support the notion that he prunes his organisation when required.

TEMPORAL NEMONIKS

Table 12 illustrates that the three exhaustive temporal nemoniks of time are *act, wait, and prepare.*

Table 12: Temporal nemoniks

- Nemonik thinking
  - Mind
    - Conscious
      - Rational thinking
        - OBJECTIVE-1
        - COLLECTIVE-2
    - Subconscious
      - Affectorial thinking
        - CREATIVE-3
        - REACTIVE-4
  - Reality
    - Space
      - ADVANCE-5
      - STAY-6
      - RETREAT-7
    - Matter
      - ACCUMULATE-8
      - PRESERVE-9
      - DISPOSE-10
    - Time
      - **ACT-11**
      - **WAIT-12**
      - **PREPARE-13**
  - Interaction
    - Perception
      - ACCEPT-14
      - REJECT-15
    - Projection
      - REVEAL-16
      - CONCEAL-17

TEMPORAL NEMONIK 11—ACT

Act is the temporal nemonik that prompts the mind to change or move matter in space and time. Action is restricted to the present because the past is gone and the future is not here yet. Action involves often risks, but without risks, you are unlikely to reach your goals. Hence, action is a trade-off between risk-avoidance and risk-taking.

Keywords for *act* include: *accept, accumulate, advance, carry out, conceal, create, dispose, do, execute, go, memorize, move, perform, prepare, preserve, react, recall, reject, respond, retreat, reveal, rule, stay, wait, etc.*[92]

Lao Zi wrote—*In action, the goodness is timing.*[93] Timing is the execution of an action at the most productive moment. An emergency could force you into action without sufficient preparation. Such actions might foster panic and rashness. Panic is a counterproductive conflict for mental dominance between the conscious and subconscious that paralyses the mind. During a panic attack, a perceived threat hyper-activates the conscious so that experience stored in the subconscious mindsets cannot be used. Furthermore, rashness is making fast but counterproductive decisions without adequate conscious thoughts or subconscious mindsets. Rashness stops the conflict for mental dominance between the conscious and subconscious because the dices are thrown. Hence, rashness is often a concealed attempt to inhibit a panic attack. In contrast, proactivity is based on the idea that prevention is the best cure. Proactivity is a productive early action that fosters opportunities and inhibits threats.

Every action evokes a reaction. Are you prepared for the inevitable reaction to your action? Starting a fight that you cannot finish is a threat. In accord, Sun Zi warned—*Never underestimate your opponent.*[94]

Sir Richard and action

Sir Richard focuses on the present, leaves the past behind, and does not worry too much about the future.[95] The extensive advance of the Virgin brand and the great accumulation of matter in a relatively short time, suggests that Sir Richard is decisive and knows when, where, and how to act.[96] Despite his many successes, he was sometimes forced into action. For example, he started the mail-order business to save Student Magazine and the Student Advisory Centre; opened retail shops to save the mail-order business; closed down Event Magazine due to competition; abandoned the takeover of EMI due to cash-flow problems; and sold Virgin Music in order to save Virgin Atlantic.[97] However, Sir Richard's action was correctly timed when he sold Sega before the market in computer games collapsed.[98] He also earned an extra £10 million by taking the option to receive the money for Virgin Music immediately.[99] His actions are characterized by surprise, initiative, speed, determination, priorities, intuition, impulses, and momentum.[100]

TEMPORAL NEMONIK 12—WAIT

Wait is the temporal nemonik that prompts the mind to delay an action until it is the right time for that action.

Keywords for *wait* include: *adjourn, break, breather, defer, delay, patience, pause, postpone, procrastinate, put on hold, recess, respite, rest, stand, stall, suspend, time off, timeout, timing, etc.*

Patience is crucial for the correct timing of waiting. However, it is not in your interest to wait if you are not sufficiently prepared. In that case, it is more effective to spend your time on preparations. Furthermore, waiting could become stagnation. Waiting creates also opportunities for your opponents. In general, wait when the conditions are likely to improve and act when they are likely to get worse. Nevertheless, while you are waiting, your opponents might regroup and manoeuvre into a better position. Waiting might also hide personal procrastination and cowardice. Procrastination is a counterproductive delay of action that inhibits opportunities and fosters threats.

Sir Richard and waiting

Sir Richard waited to the last moment to sell Virgin Music and take successfully British Airways to court.[101] Furthermore, he earned nine million pounds by following Ken Berry's advice to wait for a better exchange rate concerning the payment to Fujisankei.[102] Again, with my perfect hindsight, it is easy to see that waiting to sell the failing MCEG was counterproductive.[103]

TEMPORAL NEMONIK 13—PREPARE

Prepare is the temporal nemonik that prompts the mind to get ready for action.

Keywords for *prepare* include: *analysing, decision-making, fostering leadership, internalizing nemonik thinking, learning, marketing, mind management, negotiating, organizing, planning, positioning, prioritizing, promotion, risk-management, setting goals, time-management, training, etc.*

As they say—*Prepare for the worst and hope for the best.* Planning is an exhaustive examination of the spatial, material, temporal, perceptive, and projective aspects of reality with the four mindmodes in order to create a plan. A plan is a mental or physical map describing the intended actions across time required to reach a predetermined goal. Plans include strategies and tactics. A strategy is a plan to complete a mission, while a tactic is a plan to reach a target.

In terms of Sun Zi, positioning is the ability to manoeuvre into a situation where the strategic advantage is so large that the opposition has to avoid a conflict at all cost.[104] For nemonik thinking, opposition is anything that blocks your advance towards your goals. Hence, it does not have to be an enemy. Even your own state of mind could block you from reaching your goals. However, Sun Zi's principle of positioning remains the same—manoeuvre without force into a superior position. So, prepare your mind with nemonik thinking before you need a better way of thinking. However, preparation without action produces waste.

Some people might advise you to reduce your stress by living in the *Now*, which implies that no preparation for the future is necessary. However, that approach to life rejects *a priori* the nemoniks to *advance* into the future and *retreat* into the past. This bias fosters static thinking in a dynamic reality. Reality will always change and, therefore, such a philosophy is doomed to become counterproductive sooner or later. Reality shows that the status quo of the *Now* cannot be preserved.

I wonder how living in the *Now* would work for a prisoner in a concentration camp. Focussing on a *Now* that is saturated with deprivation, humiliation, imminent death, guard dogs, electric razor wire, and machine guns will not foster mental health or survival. That focus would not maximize your success. It would be more productive to survive on a diet of good memories from the past, while preparing plans for a future escape. Imagine your future self, walking hand in hand with your partner.

The future is a continuous string of *Now*'s and, therefore, we have to prepare right now for those *Now*'s. Furthermore, if you live in a negative *Now*, then you might have focussed in the past too much on the *Now*. At that time, you might have ignored your experiences of the past and the predictability of the future. For example, in a past *Now*, the hypothetical prisoner might have been able to avoid the concentration camp by preparing for the future. The prisoner was caught because he focused in the past too much on the *Now*, while the status quo of that *Now* could not be preserved. Are you still with me?

The conscious focuses mainly on the *Now*, while the subconscious is more concerned with the past and future. Hence, a bias towards the *Now* fosters conscious rational thinking and inhibits subconscious affectorial thinking. This would considerably reduce your mindpower because your genius lives in your subconscious. Inhibiting your subconscious will also inhibit affecters that signal potential subconscious problems. Ignoring affecters such as anxiety, depression, pain, and stress by living consciously in the *Now*, will not solve those problems.[105] In contrast, it will allow them to fester until a mental breakdown becomes inevitable. It is like taking a painkiller to reduce the pain from placing your hand on a hot stove. Pain is an affecter that urges you to remove your hand. Ignoring that affecter is counterproductive. The painkiller might inhibit the affecter, but it will not solve the underlying problem. Although you might not feel it, your hand will still burn to a useless crisp.[106]

Nemonik thinkers are dynamic thinkers and, therefore, their conscious focus is determined by the situation. In some situations, it is productive to focus on the present. In other situations, it might be more productive to focus on the past or future. Nemonik thinkers deal with all affecters, independent whether they concern the past, present, or future. The experience of the past is the basis for preparation in the present, which might reduce anxiety, depression, pain, and stress in the future.[107] Preparation could turn current weaknesses into future strengths, while revealing opportunities and removing threats.

Perfection comes at a high cost. Sometimes, perfection is a necessity. However, the 80/20 rule holds that in 20% of the time required to do a perfect job, people are able to complete 80% of that job to a reasonable standard. The remaining 80% of their time will be spent on perfecting the last 20% of that job. If the rule applies, then you could complete 80% of five jobs to a reasonable standard (400%) in the same time required to complete one job perfectly (100%).[108] Hence, if the quality of the jobs is limited to 80%, then the total quantity would increase from 100 to 400%. Therefore, it is productive to evaluate the need for quantity and quality—set clear goals and priorities—and use time management in order to achieve them.

Something imperfect could be still very useful. Any perfection is only perfect within a particular situation. A set of nemoniks might provide the perfect strategy for a particular situation. However, that situation will inevitably change and what was once perfect becomes imperfect. Consequently, preparing the perfect strategy is preparing the one that is a *Best Fit* for the actual situation. In accord, nemonik thinkers have not one perfect strategy. They create a strategy that fits perfectly the particular situation. Nemonik thinkers are unpredictable because they agree with Lao Zi—*Competent strategists have no strategy.*

Know what is urgent.
Know what is important.
Be aware of the difference!

Avoiding all risks is unlikely to maximize your success because you have to advance sooner or later towards your goals. On the other hand, if you take too many risks, then you might fail. Reality is confusing and rarely is there sufficient information for a clear decision. Ultimately, most decisions are judgment calls. Judgment calls are intuitive decisions about risk-avoidance and risk-taking without sufficient conscious information. Preparation is productive if it fosters proactivity, while it is counterproductive if it is used as an excuse for procrastination.

Sir Richard and preparing

Sir Richard mentions that he likes preparation.[109] In accord, he describes enthusiastically his leadership style, goal setting, planning, prioritizing, organizing, positioning, and his risk-management.

The leadership qualities that Sir Richard values include adaptation, competition, fair play, forgiveness, honesty, independence, praise, and reputation.[110] He seems to prefer, predominantly, a macro-management style, focus on priorities, delegation of authority, and personal accountability. Despite delegating tasks to others, he prefers to remain in overall control.[111] After carefully listening to others, he makes up his mind quickly and sticks to his decisions.[112]

Sir Richard fosters communication, co-operation, and unity within his organisation by maintaining a flat hierarchy of small symbiotic units, putting his employees first, maintaining an open-door policy, and fostering teamwork.[113] He does not like personal confrontations and, therefore, he bypasses people who disagree with him, delegates the disposal of employees to others, and avoids court actions.[114] Furthermore, his business philosophy is based on non-directional expansion.[115] Non-directional or organic expansion is the growth of a collective towards available opportunities without having a predetermined mission. On the other hand, directional expansion is the growth of a collective towards a predetermined mission.

Sir Richard's set himself goals that are long-term, challenging, and creative. However, he mentions that he is an idealist and that it is not his mission just to make money. For him, business is a way of life and having fun is an important part of it. This is illustrated by his balloon flights, powerboat races, and humanitarian activities.[116] We are a social species and, therefore, the ultimate significance of any mission could be measured in its benefits for other people, and especially future generations. Sir Richard's charitable and humanitarian activities could suggest an underlying altruistic mission.

Sir Richard's comments suggest that he translates suitable ideas into reliable business plans and maintains a strong focus on them. His planning is intuitive and impulsive, allowing him to make rapid decisions about people and issues.[117]

Sir Richard showed the importance of prioritizing when he ignored the financial problems with Nova Scotia in order to sign up Janet Jackson; and the problems with British Airways to sign up The Rolling Stones.[118] He focussed on the important issue of generating long-term income without being distracted by the urgent issue of short-term cash-flow problems.

Sir Richard organised the Virgin group into a people oriented organization with an organic structure. This structure features small independent units, symbiosis, and vertical integration of those units, joint-ventures, and open communication channels. Small units are more flexible than a large monolithic organisation and, therefore, they are able to take full advantage of new ideas, products, and opportunities in a wide variety of markets.[119] Sir Richard emphasizes that people are important and adheres to the motto—*Small is beautiful.*

Sir Richard positioned himself when he stalked EMI; recorded conversations to gain an advantage over British Airways; presented done-deals to his employees and board in order to circumvent their resistance; approached Saddam Hussein through the Royalty of Jordan; and moved his balloon to Miyakonojo to take advantage of the jet stream. Other examples of positioning were splitting up the Virgin Group before the flotation, and the relocation of programmers before selling the Sega license.[120] In accord with the advice of Sun Zi, Sir Richard avoids direct confrontations.[121] However, his daring approach to business, saving others, ballooning, and power boating shows substantial personal courage. Therefore, it would be a mistake to interpret his avoidance of confrontations as a weakness. More likely, he positions himself in order to reach his goals with minimal effort.

Sir Richard's risk-management includes cash-flow control, cost control, cutting losses, geographical spread, joint-ventures, limiting the downside, mutually protecting units, product diversification, small independent units, and a symbiosis of those units.[122] Sir Richard's business philosophy is based on expansion during a cash crisis. However, investments in new ventures are likely to increase short-term cash-flow problems. This notion is supported by his problems with Coutts Bank, Nova Scotia Bank, and Lloyds Bank.[123] Ultimately, overexpansion forced the abortion of the takeover of EMI and the sale of Virgin Music. The risk-management seems to have failed when MCEG crashed.[124] In accord with nemonik thinking, Sir Richard mentions that survival is the key priority.[125] Hence, the risks that a person takes should allow that person to survive and fight another day. Sir Richard did more than just survive.

Notes

INTERACTION

Table 13 illustrates that the exhaustive parts of interaction are *perception and projection*. Interaction is the effect of the mind on reality and vice versa. Reality is like a mirror that reflects your behaviour. Whatever you do affects reality, while that affected reality will affect you in return—*What goes around comes around*. It is like karma. If you are grumpy, then you are likely to perceive a grumpy world. On the other hand, if you are friendly, then you are likely to see a friendly world. Look at Sir Richard's perpetual grin! Unkindness is counterproductive. The unkind are imprisoned in an unkind world. If you feel sad, then pretend to be happy and your reality will improve. Fake it until you make it!

Be kind to the kind, because they deserve it.
Be kind to the unkind, because they need it.

People have to maximize their success within the constraints of reality. Unconditional love and pure altruism are rare. Many people provide for others in order to receive what they need for themselves. Most relationships are based on reciprocity—*I scratch your back if you scratch mine*. Hence, if you do not get what you need, then check first whether you give others what they need. Reciprocity requires negotiation. The information that is available to the negotiators determines the relative strength of their positions. Hence, information management is important. It is the ability to manage the perception and projection of information in order to maximize your success. In that way, nemonik thinkers turn weaknesses into strengths, and threats into opportunities.

Table 13: Parts of interaction				
Nemonik thinking				
	Mind			
		Conscious		
			Rational thinking	
				OBJECTIVE-1
				COLLECTIVE-2
		Subconscious		
			Affectorial thinking	
				CREATIVE-3
				REACTIVE-4
	Reality			
			Space	
				ADVANCE-5
				STAY-6
				RETREAT-7
			Matter	
				ACCUMULATE-8
				PRESERVE-9
				DISPOSE-10
			Time	
				ACT-11
				WAIT-12
				PREPARE-13
	Interaction			
			Perception	
				ACCEPT-14
				REJECT-15
			Projection	
				REVEAL-16
				CONCEAL-17

Perception

Perception is the part of interaction that manages the incoming information flow from the sensory reality towards the mind. Listening is an easy way to obtain information because most people prefer to talk and search continuously for willing listeners. Look at the success of social media such as Youtube, Twitter, and Facebook. People just keep talking even when no one is listening. Furthermore, individuals and businesses use detectives to spy on each other, governments use intelligence agencies, and the military has its drones, spies, scouts, and satellites. Furthermore, scientists try to discover information that is hidden in nature, while hackers seek access to information that is hidden in computers. Perception is managed by applying the exhaustive nemoniks to *accept and reject* information.

Those who speak do not listen.
Those who do not listen do not learn.
Those who do not learn do not know.
Those who do not know should not speak.

Projection

Projection is the part of interaction that refers to managing the outgoing information flow from the mind towards the sensory reality. Projection is predominantly under your control and the quality of your projection will determine your reputation. News media, intelligence agencies, public relation agents, and spin-doctors have made projection their profession. Furthermore, the projection of gossip provides a living for tabloids, while ruining many reputations at the same time. Projection is managed by applying the exhaustive nemoniks to *reveal and conceal* information.

Be careful what you project.
You can lose your reputation only once.

Notes

PERCEPTUAL NEMONIKS

Table 14 illustrates that the exhaustive perceptual nemoniks are *accept and reject.*

Table 14: Perceptual nemoniks				
Nemonik thinking				
	Mind			
		Conscious		
			Rational thinking	
				OBJECTIVE-1
				COLLECTIVE-2
		Subconscious		
			Affectorial thinking	
				CREATIVE-3
				REACTIVE-4
	Reality			
			Space	
				ADVANCE-5
				STAY-6
				RETREAT-7
			Matter	
				ACCUMULATE-8
				PRESERVE-9
				DISPOSE-10
			Time	
				ACT-11
				WAIT-12
				PREPARE-13
	Interaction			
			Perception	
				ACCEPT-14
				REJECT-15
			Projection	
				REVEAL-16
				CONCEAL-17

PERCEPTUAL NEMONIK 14—ACCEPT

Accept is the perceptual nemonik that prompts the mind to accept the incoming information as a true description of the sensory reality.

Keywords for *accept* include: *accord, agree, approve, believe, careless, comply, confident, converted, convinced, credulous, faith, gullible, incoming information, influenced, lax criterion, naive, perception, persuaded, susceptible, swayed, true, trust, etc.*

It is often very difficult to decide whether information is either true or false. As Byron wrote—*The truth is often stranger than fiction.* When you adopt a lax decision criterion, then you will accept information easily. Be warned—*The incompetent soon believe what they desire to be true (Proverb).* The advantage of such a lax criterion is that you accept most of the true information. On the other hand, the disadvantage of a lax decision criterion is that you accept too much false information and become too trusting and gullible. Often, the lies sound even better than the truth in order to influence your decisions. As they say—*If it looks too good to be true, then it probably is.* The gullible might fall into traps or are ambushed by their opponents.

Sir Richard and accepting

Sir Richard fosters an open-door policy that provides him with grassroots information about his organization.[126] He accepted external information from Randolph Fields to start Virgin Atlantic; Prince Rupert to sign The Rolling Stones; Gerry Spencer for Virgin Cola; and from Rowan Gormley to enter the financial-services industry. Furthermore, Sir Richard accepted information obtained by Chris Hutchins concerning that person's conversation with Brian Basham in relation to British Airways. In addition, Sir Richard wore a hidden microphone to record his conversation with a contact providing information about investigations by British Airways about the Virgin Group.[127] On the other hand, he regretted accepting a tape containing conversations between representatives of British Airways.[128] Apparently, accepting information about the financial situation of MCEG and buying another publishing house was counterproductive.[129] However, failure and mistakes are inevitably part of a rewarding life. If we try to avoid all risks, we cannot maximize our success. In accord, Sir Richard manages his risks and accepts the consequences.

PERCEPTUAL NEMONIK 15—REJECT

Reject is the perceptual nemonik that prompts the mind to refuse the incoming information as a true description of the sensory reality.

Keywords for *reject* include: *careful, decline, disaccord, disagree, disapprove, disbelieve, discontent, distrust, excluding, false, incoming information, perception, rebel, refuse, revolt, strict criterion, unconventional, unconvinced, untrue, etc.*

When a person adopts a strict decision criterion, then that person will reject information easily. They follow the advice—*Believe nothing of what you hear and only half of what you see (Proverb).* The advantage of such a strict criterion is that you reject most of the false information. On the other hand, the disadvantage is that you reject too much true information and become paranoid. Nevertheless, even paranoid people might be followed.

Sir Richard and rejecting

Sir Richard's organisation was strengthened by his rejection of the objections of Simon Draper and Ken Berry against film-making and starting Virgin Atlantic. He also rejected the perception held by many in the music industry that the days of The Rolling Stones were over; the advice of his wife Joan and Peter Gabriel not to sell Virgin Music; the objections of Trevor Abbott and Ken Berry to the flotation of Virgin; and Don Cruickshank's opinion about a management buyout. Furthermore, he rejected proposals to limit the use of the Virgin brand-name. His rejection of a proposal to become an underwriter of Lloyds Insurance is likely to have saved him a considerable amount of money. Sir Richard also mentioned that he rejects information from private detectives.[130] By rejecting information, one is likely to reject inadvertently some good opportunities. In accord, Sir Richard admits that he rejected the board-game Trivial Pursuit and a wind-up radio.[131] However, those rejections appear indeed trivial viewed in the light of his success.

PROJECTIONAL NEMONIKS

Table 15 illustrates that the exhaustive projectional nemoniks are *reveal and conceal.*

Table 15: Projectional nemoniks

Nemonik thinking				
	Mind			
		Conscious		
			Rational thinking	
				OBJECTIVE-1
				COLLECTIVE-2
		Subconscious		
			Affectorial thinking	
				CREATIVE-3
				REACTIVE-4
	Reality			
			Space	
				ADVANCE-5
				STAY-6
				RETREAT-7
			Matter	
				ACCUMULATE-8
				PRESERVE-9
				DISPOSE-10
			Time	
				ACT-11
				WAIT-12
				PREPARE-13
	Interaction			
			Perception	
				ACCEPT-14
				REJECT-15
			Projection	
				REVEAL-16
				CONCEAL-17

PROJECTIONAL NEMONIK 16—REVEAL

Reveal is the projectional nemonik that prompts the mind to project true information to the sensory reality.

Keywords for *reveal* include: *advertise, allies, associates, careless, confident, clear, disclose, divulge, explain, explicit, expose, friends, gossip, honest, inform, lax criterion, loyal, manifest, network, notify, open, outgoing information, overt, partners, plain, projection, promote, publish, release, slip, supporters, tell, transparent, trust, warning, etc.*

Sometimes, you will have to reveal information, because if competence is silent, then incompetence will rule. You might reveal true information to your allies in order to strengthen the alliance. However, revealing carries the threat that others use that information against you. As they say—*Confess and be hanged.* Nevertheless, the truth is often easier to defend than lies because lies have the tendency to become increasingly complex. On the other hand, you might reveal true information to your opponents in order to threaten them with your strength. Whatever you decide—*Do not wash your dirty linen in public (Proverb).*

Sir Richard and revealing

Sir Richard reveals exhaustive information about his life and work in his autobiography. His comments suggest that his promotional skills have been vital to his success. He used balloon flights, powerboat races, and dress ups to promote the *Virgin* brand.[132] Sir Richard's networking skills are evident from the index of his book that reads like a *Who's Who?* Compared to the number of topics mentioned in his index, the number of people is substantial and includes Princess Diana of Wales, Vanessa Redgrave, Margaret Thatcher, Sir Edward Heath, and King Hussein and Queen Noor of Jordan.[133]

Revealing information backfired sometimes for Sir Richard. In his attempt to sell Student Magazine to IPC, he revealed his plans for the future of the magazine, which terminated the negotiations. Telling Mike Oldfield that the profit from his records was needed to finance less successful artists had also a negative effect. Furthermore, revealing the truth is not always easy. Sir Richard mentions that he tried several times to reveal the truth about British Airways.[134]

The managing director of Arista found out the hard way that revealing too much information is counterproductive. He boasted to Sir Richard that he would sign the French pop star Julien Clerc. As a result, Sir Richard signed the artist before Arista could complete its negotiations.[135]

PROJECTIONAL NEMONIK 17—CONCEAL

Conceal is the projectional nemonik that prompts the mind to project false information to the sensory reality.

Keywords for *conceal* include: *ambush, avoid, camouflage, careful, cloak, confuse, covert, deceitful, deception, disguise, dishonest, disinformation, dissimulation, distortion, enemy, ensnare, front, insincere, dishonest, disloyal, distrust, false, hide, hostile, lie, mask, misinformation, obscure, opponents, outgoing information, projection, screen, secret, spin, strict criterion, trap, undercover, underground, undisclosed, untrue, withhold, etc.*

You could conceal true information from your opponents in order to trap them or lure them into an ambush. Concealing information could be also used to bypass opposition and present your opponents with a done deal. However, concealing information from your allies might harm your credibility and their precious support. Dissimulation and counter claims are ways to create confusion that could conceal the truth. However, the truth is often difficult to hide—*When the mind plots deceit, then the body projects betrayal.*

Whistle-blowers and news media show also that the truth is very hard to conceal. Simple lies have the tendency to become complex ones. Liars are more likely to fail because they have to remember that complexity. For example, the US President Richard Nixon attempted to hide his involvement in the busted Watergate burglary. At the end, Watergate became his Waterloo.

Sir Richard and concealing

Sir Richard mentions that he dislikes criticizing and confronting people.[136] This might be the reason that he conceals information from them. Alternatively, it is an effective way to bypass opposition, which reduces the time and effort required to overcome such obstacles. Sir Richard concealed information from Nik Powell about purchasing two nightclubs; from Don Cruickshank about the management buyout of Virgin; and from his board about opening the Megastore in Paris. Furthermore, he concealed information about the sale of Virgin Music to EMI from Peter Gabriel and Virgin's employees.[137]

Concealing information from his organization seems to contradict Sir Richard's policies to put his employees first, have an open-door policy, and foster teamwork.[138] However, he explains that if the truth about the financial problems of Virgin had been leaked, then it might have caused irreparable damage to the confidence in Virgin's solvency.[139] For the same reason, he concealed the truth about the financial state of Virgin from the public by attacking rumours in the *New Musical Express*. He also concealed his intensions to sign the singer Julien Clerc, and knowledge that conversations concerning British Airways would be recorded.[140]

Notes

APPLYING NEMONIK THINKING

Applying nemonik thinking involves—memorizing the 17 nemoniks, setting goals, nemonik analyses, nemonik acceleration, nemonik meditation, and inner-team visualization.

MEMORIZE THE 17 NEMONIKS

Table 17 shows the nemonik template. If you want to maximize your success, then it is in your interest to memorize the seventeen nemoniks that form the nemonik template. That template will defragment your memory and, therefore, it will improve the storage and recall of information. Furthermore, it will accelerate your thinking and prevent mental blindspots.

Table 17: Nemonik template

- Nemonik thinking
  - Mind
    - Conscious
      - Rational thinking
        - **OBJECTIVE-1**
        - **COLLECTIVE-2**
    - Subconscious
      - Affectorial thinking
        - **CREATIVE-3**
        - **REACTIVE-4**
  - Reality
    - Space
      - **ADVANCE-5**
      - **STAY-6**
      - **RETREAT-7**
    - Matter
      - **ACCUMULATE-8**
      - **PRESERVE-9**
      - **DISPOSE-10**
    - Time
      - **ACT-11**
      - **WAIT-12**
      - **PREPARE-13**
  - Interaction
    - Perception
      - **ACCEPT-14**
      - **REJECT-15**
    - Projection
      - **REVEAL-16**
      - **CONCEAL-17**

Definition nemoniks

Objective—mental nemonik that deals with the natural order of the sensory reality, which can be described by natural laws and facts that make nature predictable.

Collective —mental nemonik that generates artificial rules, which determine the rights and obligations of individuals within a collective, and makes their behaviours predictable.

Creative—mental nemonik that deals with the chaos of reality by generating creative affecters.

Reactive—mental nemonik that deals with the chaos of reality by habituating mindsets that generate reactive affecters.

Advance—spatial nemonik that prompts the mind to decrease the distance to the goal.

Stay—spatial nemonik that prompts the mind to maintain the same distance to the goal.

Retreat—spatial nemonik that prompts the mind to increase the distance to the goal.

Accumulate—material nemonik that prompts the mind to increase the amount of matter that is under control.

Preserve—material nemonik that prompts the mind to maintain the same amount of matter that is under control.

Dispose—material nemonik that prompts the mind to decrease the amount of matter that is under control.

Act—temporal nemonik that prompts the mind to change or move matter in space and time.

Wait—temporal nemonik that prompts the mind to delay an action until it is the right time for that action.

Prepare—temporal nemonik that prompts the mind to get ready for action.

Accept—perceptual nemonik that prompts the mind to accept the incoming information as a true description of the sensory reality.

Reject—perceptual nemonik that prompts the mind to refuse the incoming information as a true description of the sensory reality.

Reveal—projectional nemonik that prompts the mind to project true information to the sensory reality.

Conceal—projectional nemonik that prompts the mind to project false information to the sensory reality.

Operational nemoniks—thirteen nemoniks including the nine reality and four interactive nemoniks.

Nemonik thinking is like using a mental chest of seventeen drawers. Each nemonik is a key to a drawer and it is up to you what you put in these drawers. A drawer could contain advice, assumptions, beliefs, examples, facts, ideas, questions, and warnings that are associated with that particular nemonik. By consciously recalling a particular nemonik, your memory will recall automatically strings of associated information from the corresponding drawer. For example, the nemonik to *advance* might bring already to mind some of the previously mentioned keywords such as attack, charge, chase, develop, expand, forward, invade, offense, progress, promote, etc. The depth of your nemonik thinking depends on the quantity and quality of the information that you have stored in the nemonik drawers of your memory. Therefore, it is in your interest to study my other books such as *Glossary for Nemonik Thinking*; *Dictionary for Nemonik Thinking*; *Sun Zi's Strategies for Nemonik Thinkers*, and *Lao Zi's Principle for Nemonik Thinkers.*[viii]

The memory uses the nemonik template also as a mnemonic to guide the process of thinking by recalling each nemonik one-by-one for the actual problem. This will reduce the likelihood of mental blind-spots. Furthermore, the preparedness provided by the nemonik template will accelerate your thinking and reduce your stress levels during emergencies.

[viii] Appendices.

SETTING GOALS

Never let an urge to win a competition distract you from maximizing your success. *Success is to obtain what you seek and escape what you suffer (Lao Zi).* Therefore, the crucial question is—What do you want to obtain and what do you want to escape? Determine what success means for you, because success is a personal experience. Ultimately, success is an affecter. No one else can tell you what to do because this is about your success. Follow your heart and listen to your head! Life is reasonably fair because if you ask for nothing, then that is exactly what you will get. Without direction, there is little reason to move because you might waste your resources by going around in circles.

People often obtain what they seek, but then they do not like what they have obtained. Others escape the things that they need most. Dependent on the actual situation, your goal might be a long-term mission, while at other times it might be more productive to pursue short-term opportunities or escape immediate threats. Nevertheless, it is always in your interest to maximize your success. The only resource you need is your mind and the only tool you need is nemonik thinking.

NEMONIK ANALYSES

Mindmode-analysis

The value of each nemonik depends exclusively on its suitability for the actual situation. Therefore, each nemonik should be evaluated for each situation. Any bias towards or against the use of a particular nemonik fosters static thinking is a dynamic universe. Static thinkers will fail inevitably, because the favourable situation will change inevitably.

The mindmode-analysis is the core of nemonik thinking. It evaluates the exhaustive interactions of the four mental nemoniks[ix] with the thirteen operational nemoniks[x] in order to find the nemoniks that provide the *Best Fit* for the actual situation. For example, you could ask yourself how an *advance* could be affected by natural laws, collective artificial rules, creativity, and reactivity. Hence, those interactions provide instantaneously 52 options to evaluate any situation.[141]

Advance * objective
Advance * collective
Advance * creative
Advance * reactive
Stay * objective
Stay * collective
Stay * creative
Stay * reactive
Retreat * objective
Etc.

[ix] Objective, collective, creative, and reactive.

[x] Advance, stay, retreat, accumulate, preserve, dispose, act, wait, prepare, accept, reject, reveal, and conceal.

SWOT-analysis

If you want to maximize the probability of success, then it is also in your interest to apply a SWOT-analysis, which was introduced by the American business consultant Albert S. Humphrey (1926-2005). A SWOT-analysis is a problem-solving tool that evaluates the *Strengths, Weaknesses, Opportunities, and Threats* of each nemonik in comparison to the actual situation. *Strength* is an intrinsic advantage; *Weakness* is an intrinsic disadvantage; *Opportunity* is a potential advantage; and *Threat* is a potential disadvantage. For example, having a university degree is a strength, but receiving a job offer is an opportunity. Having thin bones is a weakness, but the possibility of breaking a leg during skiing is a threat.

In accord with the aim of nemonik thinking, a SWOT-analysis of each nemonik fosters the generation of questions and ideas associated with that nemonik. For example, the strength of an *advance* is approaching your goal, while a weakness is entering unknown territory. An *advance* might also provide the opportunity to surprise your opponent, or alternatively, the threat is that you might run into an ambush. Hence, the interactions between the thirteen operational nemoniks and the four SWOT components provide another 52 options to evaluate a particular situation.[142] This increases the versatility and depth of nemonik thinking.

Advance * strength
Advance * weakness
Advance * opportunity
Advance * threat
Stay * strength
Stay * weakness
Stay * opportunity
Stay * threat
Retreat * strength
Etc.

Basic SWOT-analysis

Objective—Strength: predicting nature. Weakness: infinite maze of details, increasing specialism, and decreasing communication. Opportunity: scientific progress. Threat: inhibiting compassion.

Collective—Strength: predicting people. Weakness: rebellion and conflict. Opportunity: co-operation. Threat: group-think causing collective stagnation.

Creative—Strength: dealing with the unknown future. Weakness: unrealism. Opportunity: inhibiting stagnation. Threat: unrealism.

Reactive—Strength: learning from the past. Weakness: different internal realities. Opportunity: personal perfection. Threat: cognitive dissonance causing individual stagnation.

Advance—Strength: decreases the distance to the goal. Weakness: extends supply lines. Opportunity: initiative and momentum. Threat: moving to a position that allows no stay.

Stay—Strength: inhibits risk of movement. Weakness: inhibits initiative and momentum. Opportunity: protects investment. Threat: predictability.

Retreat—Strength: preserves resources. Weakness: increase distance to goal. Opportunity: regroup. Threat: chaos.

Accumulate—Strength: obtain survival buffer. Weakness: cost of accumulation. Opportunity: spatial, material, temporal options. Threat: accumulation for accumulation's sake.

Preserve—Strength: maintain survival buffer. Weakness: cost of preserving. Opportunity: protect resources. Threat: entropy.

Dispose—Strength: efficiency. Weakness: loss investments. Opportunity: reducing cost of preserving. Threat: loss irreplaceable resources.

Act—Strength: turns ideas into reality. Weakness: show intentions. Opportunity: proactivity. Threat: impatience.

Wait—Strength: timing. Weakness: cost. Opportunity: strategical advantage. Threat: procrastination.

Prepare—Strength: positioning. Weakness: cost. Opportunity: turn weakness into strength. Threat: paralysing by analysing.

Accept—Strength: receiving all true information. Weakness: receiving too much false information. Opportunity: fosters alliances. Threat: fosters gullibility.

Reject—Strength: discards all false information. Weakness: discard too much true information. Opportunity: reality-check. Threat: inhibits alliances.

Reveal—Strength: fosters alliances. Weakness: inhibits surprise. Opportunity: fosters compassion. Threat: fosters vulnerability.

Conceal—Strength: fosters surprise. Weakness: inhibits alliances. Opportunity: fosters a trap. Threat: others reveal what you conceal.

Mindmode and SWOT-analyses

Furthermore, you could evaluate each operational nemonik with combinations of mindmode and SWOT-analysis. In that case, the interactions between the thirteen operational nemoniks versus the four mindmodes and four SWOT components provide 208 options to evaluate a particular situation.[143] At least, you will always know what to do. You better get to work.

Advance * objective * strength
Advance * objective * weakness
Advance * objective * opportunity
Advance * objective * threat
Advance * collective * strength
Advance * collective * weakness
Advance * collective * opportunity
Advance * collective * threat
Advance * creative * strength
Etc.

NEMONIK ACCELERATOR

As you know, Hegel's dialectic shows that knowledge is a process, rather than a state. As a result, nemonik thinkers assume that they are always incorrect and have to improve their thinking. They apply the nemonik accelerator in order to prevent individual and collective mental stagnation. As mentioned previously, the nemonik accelerator is a cognitive method that increases the speed of your thinking by fostering agreement during disagreement, while fostering disagreement during agreement. The nemonik accelerator reduces the counterproductive effects of groupthink and cognitive dissonance. Groupthink is a collective mental process rejecting correct information in order to protect incorrect information that is already accepted by the collective as true. Cognitive dissonance is an individual mental process rejecting correct information in order to protect the incorrect information that is already accepted by the subconscious of that individual as true. Groupthink and cognitive dissonance foster failure, because they maintain static thinking in a dynamic universe.

As mentioned previously, static thinking is a rigid way of thinking that does not adjusts to the actual situation. As a result, static thinkers are forced to adjust the situation to their particular way of thinking. Therefore, static thinking is conflict oriented and is associated with aggression, control, effort, and force. Nevertheless, reality is dynamic and sooner or later, the situation will change inevitably. At that moment, any previously productive nemoniks are likely to become counterproductive and static thinkers will fail.

If you want to maximize your success, then you need the nemonik accelerator in order to adjust your way of thinking to the actual situation. That accelerator will increase the speed of your thinking by fostering agreement during disagreement, while fostering disagreement during agreement. Therefore, you will have no need to maintain the status quo by force. You just adjust your thinking to the situation, like sailors who adjust their sails to the wind.

NEMONIK MEDITATION

The unmanaged mind is like a wild horse that has no focus and goes wherever it wants to go on the spur of the moment. It is easily distracted and changes direction without any reason. It jumps where it should tread carefully. It follows desires, rather than needs. Unconnected thoughts come and go on the screen of the conscious creating a chaos during the day that keeps the victim awake at night. Such a mental turmoil affects the surrounding reality and its counterproductive feedback leaves internally a trail of anxiety, confusion, depression, and frustration.[144]

Some sufferers try to escape from the chaos by taking a variety of chemicals that change their perception of reality. Others swap their unproductive coping strategies for equally unproductive philosophies. They hide in the now, at the cost of the past that has created them and from a future that could provide them with hope and opportunities. Too scared to face where they came from and too much disappointed to care where they are going. Many create as much noise as possible to mask the increasingly louder feedback signals from the protesting reality. In one way or another, those escapees chose a suspended animation above the turmoil of real life. Nevertheless, reality pulls them inevitably back into orbit because their behaviour does not improve their internal reality in a productive way. Underlying their turmoil is a lack of proper mind management. Mind management is the conscious management of the subconscious mind.

If you do not take the time and effort to understand your horse, then you should not complain about a rough ride. To enjoy the ride, the horse has to be taught with patience, understanding, and kindness how to respond. Similarly, you need to teach your mind how to respond to reality. Nemonik thinking provides the tools, because it is based on a dynamic model of the mind. Furthermore, the nemonik template helps to interact with reality in a productive way because the seventeen nemoniks include all the perceived aspects of the mind, reality, and their interaction. It provides a simple map comprising landmarks for navigating the infinite maze of details that comprises reality. It is up to you to manage your mind with the patience, understanding, and the kindness that it deserves.[145]

As mentioned previously, conscious dominance is a healthy state of mind that is fostered by concentration. In contrast, subconscious dominance is a healthy state of mind that is fostered by relaxation. Furthermore, semiconscious dominance is a healthy state of mind that is fostered by meditation. A mental state is a distinct level of awareness such as conscious dominance, subconscious dominance, semiconscious dominance, and unconsciousness.

In order to manage the mind, one has to learn to slide from one mental state to another. Sliding is the mental process of shifting consciously the dominance window across the mental continuum. Concentration and relaxation move the dominance window respectively to the conscious and subconscious extremes of the mental continuum. In contrast, meditation fosters a semiconscious dominance that balances those extremes. In that way, it opens the communication channel between the conscious and subconscious.

If you want to learn new tasks, provide direction to your life, and manage the subconscious then you have to concentrate in order to slide to conscious dominance. On the other hand, if you need mental and physical recuperation, then you should relax in order to slide to subconscious dominance. Furthermore, if you decide to improve your affecters, then you should meditate in order to slide to semiconscious dominance.

Semiconscious dominance is crucial for mind management. It is a natural mental state and everyone experiences it each day in one way or another. Hence, there is nothing mysterious about it. Semiconscious dominance could range from a light relaxed mental state to a deep trance. During semiconscious dominance, your conscious awareness of the sensory reality might change. People use a wide array of words to describe this mental state such as alpha, calm, contemplative, cool, dozy, drowsy, enlightened, high, inspirational, introspective, meditative, peaceful, relaxed, satori, serene, silent mind, spaced-out, trance, tranquil, twilight, zone, etc.

Semiconscious dominance occurs involuntarily during absent-mindedness, falling asleep, reading, relaxation, watching a video, repetitive tasks, snoozing, waking up, etc. It can also occur involuntarily when you are wide-awake and your subconscious reactive mindmode takes control in order to cope with an emergency. For example, your subconscious might have hit the brakes of your car before you are even consciously aware of any danger. In such emergencies, your subconscious acts and your conscious becomes an observer. This is the action with a silent mind as strived for in Eastern martial arts. Hence, semiconscious dominance might be either a state of tranquillity or high-octane action.

Semiconscious dominance is fostered voluntarily by reducing simultaneously conscious and subconscious dominance. This is achieved by meditation, recreation, relaxation, and rhythmic repetitions such as chanting, dancing, drumming, and even walking. Special techniques include autogenic training, biofeedback, mind-control, nemonik meditation, progressive relaxation, Yoga, Zen meditation, etc. Biofeedback is a learning process to control consciously an auditory or optical feedback signal that represents a subconsciously regulated physiological process. Studies have shown that it fosters the conscious control of skin temperature, brainwaves, and heart rate.[146]

Table 16: Sliding window of mental dominance

CONSCIOUS	SUBCONSCIOUS
CONCENTRATE Conscious dominance Learn new tasks	
MEDITATE Semiconscious dominance Improve affecters	
	RELAX Subconscious dominance Recuperate

Table 16 visualizes the sliding window of mental dominance. That hypothetical window determines the mental state by sliding over the mental continuum, which ranges from the conscious to the subconscious. The table shows that semiconscious dominance is crucial for maximizing your success, because it is the communication channel between your conscious and subconscious. Semiconscious dominance allows you to access consciously subconscious information, maximize mental speed and accuracy, deploy subconscious mindpower, modify counterproductive mindsets, and foster intentionally the reception of creative and reactive affecters.

Concentration and relaxation slide the dominance window in opposite directions along the mental continuum. The more you experience your subconscious, the less you experience your conscious and vice versa. When you wake up and concentrate, then your dominance window slides from the subconscious to the conscious. In contrast, when you relax and fall asleep the opposite occurs. Hence, both concentration and relaxation could evoke periods of semiconscious dominance during the transfer from one mental extreme to the other.

The conscious is mainly the mono-tasking part of your mind. In contrast, the larger subconscious is predominantly the multi-tasking part of your mind. The subconscious can activate several mindsets without conscious involvement. For instance, your subconscious can simultaneously operate a car, scratch your face, follow the GPS-directions, brake for a pedestrian crossing the road, and talk to a passenger. The usefulness of the conscious and subconscious depends entirely on the situation. If there is no adequate mindset for the task, then you need conscious dominance and concentration in order to learn one. If there is an adequate mindset, then semiconscious dominance might be more efficient. In that case, you need a silent conscious, because its critical approach will get in the way of activating efficiently the particular mindset.

Conventional thinkers are biased towards a conscious way of pseudo-rational thinking. Therefore, they are likely try to improve their affecters with conscious willpower. For example, they use their willpower to remove bad habits, curb their desires, produce positive feelings, or increase their creativity. Their conscious willpower requires concentration, which fosters inevitably conscious dominance. However, that conscious dominance will inhibit semiconscious dominance, which they need to improve their mindsets. Consequently, no amount of conscious willpower could improve their affecters. Their inevitable failures foster stress, depression, frustration, and anger.

In contrast, nemonik thinkers use nemonik meditation to improve their mindsets. Nemonik meditation is a special type of meditation that uses visualizations and unvoiced mantras in order to improve affecters during semiconscious dominance. Nemonik meditation is fast and hidden from others. Therefore, it can be used under all conditions. Exercises are provided in the appendix: Exercises Nemonik Meditation. Nothing mysterious—just try it out.

INNER TEAM VISUALIZATION

Visualization is a strong mental tool that could be used to create an inner team of imaginary experts. The stereotypes for the objective and collective mindmodes could be respectively a scientist and a judge. Furthermore, an inventor could symbolize the creative mindmode, while a computer programmer could represent the reactive mindmode. You could strengthen the images of your experts by giving them extraordinary features. For example, the scientist could have wild static hair like Albert Einstein; the judge could wear a gown and a large white wig; the inventor could have a head as a glowing light bulb; and the programmer could carry a tablet. Alternatively, you could imagine people you admire.

Visualize a boardroom where you chair a meeting with your experts. First, take your time to explain the actual situation to your experts in detail. Go over the details of the problem in your mind. The more they know, the better their advice will be. Ask each of them about the strengths, weaknesses, opportunities, and threats associated with each operational nemonik in relation to the situation. Imagine what they would say.

The scientist and judge are both rational thinkers who will focus on the facts. If you have no facts, then they cannot help you. Rational thinkers will try to convince the meeting with reason and logic. They are critical and will not let emotions blind their reasoning. They search for alternative explanations, concealed facts, errors, inaccuracies, incompleteness, mistakes, etc. They follow their head, rather than their heart.

The scientist will consider the effects of the unchangeable natural laws on the situation. Is this case indeed independent of what anyone believes? Do we have enough data? Can we apply statistics? Can we test the hypothesis? What about an experiment? Are we able to make observations? Is the logical argument valid and reliable? The strength of the scientist is realism, while the weakness is a lack of compassion.

The judge will evaluate how the changeable artificial rules of the collective will affect the outcome. Could we make a rule? What is the collective opinion? Is there any tradition? Do the rules apply? Can the rules be reinterpreted? Could we enforce the rules? Could we change the rules? Is there a majority for either side? The strength of the judge is creating group stability, while the weakness is stagnating the group with rules and regulations. Groupthink and peer pressure will maintain the rules and evoke stagnation.

The inventor and programmer are both affectorial thinkers who trust their affecters. Both experts are by definition non-rational because they receive neither sufficient facts nor rational explanations from their subconscious. Affectorial thinkers are non-critical and will urge the meeting to trust them. They will try to convince the meeting with self-confidence and charisma. Otherwise, they cannot use their affecters or their genius. They rely on their subconscious and, therefore, they are in touch with their intuitions and emotions. They follow their heart, rather than their head. They might point out that it is counterproductive to be factually correct, while feeling negatively about it.

The inventor will explore the unknown and, therefore, moves you out of your comfort zone. The inventor might use brainstorm and randomization of information. Put the problem upside down. The inventor might walk around the problem and make unrelated remarks about the situation. He or she is likely to propose unrealistic solutions. Nevertheless, do not interrupt the inventor with criticism. It will stop immediately the creative process. The inventor is very useful if you have no facts or experience with the situation. However, the inventor needs sufficient time to digest information and develop ideas. The inventor's weakness is unrealism.

The computer programmer writes the mental code for the mindsets that is based exclusively on experiences and skills obtained in the past. In accord, the programmer is always ready and will advise you to apply the prepared mindset. Act right now and rely on intuition, belief, common sense, heuristics, impulses, and reactions. The programmer's strength is accuracy and speed. The programmer's weaknesses are rash decisions, stagnation, and static thinking. The stagnation is maintained by cognitive dissonance.

If you want to maximize your success, then it is in your interest to manage the scientist, judge, inventor, and computer programmer as a team. Motivate them to speak up by actively listening to them. Praise them, rather than criticize them. I wish you success with your imaginary friends.

BUCKET EXAMPLE

On one of my walks through the local park, I met my friend Andrew Dodds. He is an enthusiastic gardener in many ways. That time he was gardening in the mind and wondered whether nemonik thinking could help a person without money or fame to make an impact in this world. He pointed out that many people see large problems, but feel utterly powerless to solve them because they have little status and are neither rich nor famous. Usually, I reply to such questions that I cannot solve the problems of humanity because there are just too many. I have to concentrate on my mission, which is to make people the smartest thinkers they can be. I try to give them better tools to solve their own problems. Nevertheless, how could nemonik thinking help? We were standing there with Andrew's wheelbarrow, spade, and a red bucket. He asked me a serious question and I just answered without thinking. The idea developed while I was talking.

Playing the devil's advocate, I suggested that Andrew had already too many resources. I invited him to throw the wheelbarrow and spade in the creek behind us, then fill the bucket with clean water. Next, he should ring the news media and announce his intention to walk to Somalia in order to bring the bucket of water to a child dying from thirst. I imagined that videos of his journey on social networks would ensure a worldwide audience within weeks. It could inspire thousands of people to appreciate the value of clean water. His simple red bucket could become a statement of humanity against the senseless suffering of children. In that way, Andrew would make a great impact with minimal resources. Okay, I was perhaps too enthusiastic with the disposal of the wheelbarrow. He could have used it to carry the bucket.

This bucket story is not just fantasy. If you believe in something like that, then you can do it yourself. It would give meaning to your life and you would save a child! The journey might take a year, but what a great story to tell your grandchildren. It would give a positive meaning to the expression *bucket list.* Do not wait until the end of your life to do the important things. Find your own bucket right now! Live each day as if it is the last one! The only resource you need is your mind. The only tool you need is nemonik thinking.

Bucket analysis

The following section is a mindmode-analysis of my idea to bring some water from New Zealand to a thirsty child in Somalia. The notion that a simple plastic bucket could make a significant difference in this pragmatic world was not the result of rational thinking. In contrast, it was a non-rational result of affectorial thinking.

The *objective mindmode* suggests that the idea is feasible. Given enough time, a healthy person could walk that distance with a bucket. If we are able to put a man on the moon, then we must be able to bring a bucket of water to a Somalian child. The *collective mindmode* emphasizes the need for visas and passports. Collectives along the road might offer support. The *creative mindmode* seems to be involved because the idea is not based on previous experience. It is a step into the unknown. The *reactive mindmode* made me immediately feel good about the project. I would like to support the bucket project because my intuition tells me that it is worthwhile and that it would work. The emotional gain would be substantial because it would save a child and the after effects might reduce the suffering of many innocent children. Hence, it seems that all four mindmodes were involved.

Advance—the idea entails a geographical advance to Somalia. That would lead literally into new territory with possible dangers and surprises, while the support lines of friends and family would be stretched to the limit. This would involve risks, which may convince the traveller to *stay* for a while or *retreat* altogether from the project.

Accumulate—the traveller would be in a position to accumulate donations, admiration, emotional gain, experience, fame, followers, goodwill, gratitude, importance, leadership, love, publicity, power, satisfaction, self-esteem, self-growth, status, support, etc. *Preserve* —the bucket of water and the health, fitness, and motivation of the traveller should be preserved during the journey. *Dispose*—the traveller might have to dispose of his or her current job, goals, regular income, security, spade, and wheelbarrow. To reduce the weight, the traveller could also dispose of the bucket and replace it with a symbolic water bottle. However, that might reduce the impact of the image of the water carrier.

Action—the time to act is right now because the situation for that particular child is likely to worsen. How much time has she left without water? This is action time! *Waiting* —humanity has waited too long already. Despite the heroic efforts of many people, humanity spends more money on killing people, rather than helping them. *Preparing* —this idea would provide a mission and many targets for the traveller. Other people might follow the example and take part in the journey. Alternatively, they might find their own bucket. This bucket movement could transform the traveller from a follower into a leader, fostering self-esteem and empowerment. The priority is clear because the action is both important and urgent. The child's life is in immediate danger, while the journey is likely to give great meaning to the life of the traveller. The journey could be financed by crowd funding on social media. The organization of the journey could be minimal because a pedestrian cannot carry heavy supplies. Many supporters are likely to become involved along the route. Very likely, the traveller could live off the land. With the help of social media, this journey might create a huge network for the cause and the traveller.

Accept—the traveller would have to accept the media information that there is a major drought in Africa and that help is needed. Otherwise, there would be no reason to carry the bucket all that way. *Reject*—in order to succeed, the traveller might have to reject criticism that the project will fail. Criticism can be very demotivating. Do not let them get to you.

Reveal—the traveller could reveal the intention to do something for a child in need and promote that great cause; inform the news and social media, and give interviews and put video clips of the journey on social media sites such as Facebook and YouTube; and keep people informed daily about the progress and obstacles. *Conceal*—the traveller might have to conceal any personal doubts about the mission. Expressed doubts reinforce the tendency of others to express their demotivating criticism. We all have doubts! Doubts are healthy warnings, but they should not stop us from doing what has to be done. Act as a leader—walk tall. Fake it, until you make it!

The bucket project might not be the best idea, but it illustrates that you do not need many resources to make a significant difference. The only resource you need is your mind, while the only tool you need is nemonik thinking.

WWI EXERCISE (PART II)

Exercise

Revaluate in writing the advice of your imaginary officers to—*Act right now and advance!* A comparison between your first and second evaluation will reveal your progress. Next, compare your evaluations with the following suggestions.

As you know, the mental nemoniks are *objective, collective, creative,* and *reactive.* Your objective mindmode reminds you to consider the laws of nature. Like the Romans at Masada, the advance might be literally an uphill battle so that you have to fight gravity as well.[147] Your collective mindmode reminds you to evaluate manmade rules. During the First World War, a gas attack might have supported the advance. At present, the rules of the global collective deem it criminal to use gas. Your creative mindmode might provide an original solution, like the Greeks who used a large wooden horse filled with soldiers to conquer Troy. They tricked the defenders into bringing the horse into their city. During the night, the hidden soldiers opened the gates of Troy for the Greek army. Hence, you should look even a given horse in the mouth, because everything depends on the actual situation. Furthermore, your reactive mindmode provides affecters. What was your first reaction to the advice? What does your intuition tells you? Flip a coin! If there is no time to think and there are insufficient facts, then you are forced to rely on your reactive mindmode as a general. Is that particular mindset ready? Did you memorize your nemonik template? Are you confident? Otherwise, you should have rejected the job.

The spatial nemoniks are *advance, stay,* and *retreat.* The advice to advance raises the question whether that advance would support your strategy and mission. Is this a desperate all-or-nothing action? Could you survive an unsuccessful advance? Did you question your army's ability to defend the destination of the proposed advance? Remember, the French and German advances into Russia both failed those criteria. Furthermore, the alternative spatial nemoniks remind you to stay or retreat. You could stay in the relative safety of your trenches. That was quite a popular decision in WWI. On the other hand, you could retreat in order to fight another day. A retreat would make the defences of your opponent obsolete. Pride should not stop you because it is a weakness, rather than a strategy! Question your officers—make them think!

The material nemoniks are *accumulate, preserve,* and *dispose.* The advice of your officers ignores all three nemoniks. Nevertheless, those nemoniks remind you that you might need to accumulate ammunition, preserve your lengthening supply lines, and dispose of your heavy artillery in order to speed up your advance. Did your officers manage their resources adequately? As a general, you do not need to solve all the problems, but you need to ask the right questions so that your officers will solve them.

The temporal nemoniks are *act, wait,* and *prepare.* The advice to '*act right now*' raises important questions. Why is this the right time to act? What is the competitive advantage of acting right now? What are the expected reactions of your opponents? Is your army prepared for those reactions? Remember, Sun Zi said—*Competent generals do not fight.*[148] Is there any way to manoeuvre into a stronger position without a fight? The temporal nemoniks remind you also to consider *waiting and preparing.* It might be advantageous to wait if the conditions are improving, while you might have to act if they are getting worse. Is your army sufficiently prepared to finish the advance successfully? How is their morale? Should you wait for new supplies or prepare by digging more trenches? Your staff officers should be able to answer those questions.

The perceptual nemoniks are *accept* and *reject.* Although the advice of your officers does not contain anything about information, the perceptual nemoniks remind you to obtain information. You might need to send out probing troops, skirmishers, spies, or scouts to obtain information about your opponent's position. Look for strengths, weaknesses, threats, and opportunities. Check the quality of the received information. Accepting incorrect information could lure you into a trap, while rejecting correct information could waste a vital opportunity. Did your officers reject information and concealed that information from you? Press them for answers!

The projectional nemoniks are *reveal* and *conceal.* The advice of your officers does not tell you how they project their *advance* towards the enemy. The projectional nemoniks are reminders that you could conceal your advance or reveal it as a threat. You might sneak up on your opponent in the middle of the night. Alternatively, a loud diversion in bright daylight could create a confusion that gives you a competitive advantage. Did your officers reveal accidentally any information to the enemy and concealed that from you? Project yourself as a leader. Do not focus on blame, but help your officers to think for themselves and find solutions. That is your job as a general!

The advice to '*act right now and advance*' is hopelessly inadequate because it includes only two of the seventeen nemoniks. However, the aim of this exercise is to see how many nemoniks you included in your written evaluations. Check it carefully! Each missing nemonik might indicate a mental blind-spot. Knowing those weaknesses will maximize your probability of your success.

CONVENTIONAL THINKING

Conventional thinking is an incomplete and unsystematic way of thinking that maximizes the probability of winning by applying the way of pseudo-rational thinking that is propagated by the educational system.

WINNING VERSUS SUCCESS

Nemonik thinking is a bilateral way of thinking, because it is based on both rational and affectorial thinking. On the other hand, conventional thinking is a unilateral way of thinking, because it is biased towards pseudo-rational thinking that inhibits affectorial thinking.

Aristotle's rational thinking initiated the Renaissance, and the Industrial, Biotechnical, and Informational Revolutions. Rational thinking has been the competitive advantage that made us the dominant species on Earth. It brought us to the top of the food-chain. We rule this planet. However, competition for individual resources and privileges within that new reality has corrupted the pure ways of thinking. Socrates' critical thinking is replaced by criticizing opponents, while Aristotle's rational thinking is replaced by the rationalizations of preselected conclusions. That development spawned the conventional way of thinking that is now propagated by the educational system.

Often, the word *irrational* has been used as a negative label to discredit ideas, emotions, and intuitions generated by affectorial thinkers. Conventional thinking inhibits subconscious affectorial thinking. As a result, conventional thinking has become a static way of thinking in a dynamic reality. That is a dangerous development, because your conscious is only a small tip of your mental iceberg. Your gigantic subconscious is the seat of your genius. If you want to maximize your success, then you cannot afford to ignore your genius. Furthermore, in chaotic situations, rational thinking is useless, because there are no facts to submit to reason, while the conscious is far too slow to deal with emergencies. Such conditions require adequately prepared affecters. Therefore, the inhibition of affectorial thinking is counterproductive and extremely dangerous.

Conventional thinking contains a wide variety of cognitive methods including convergent, creative, critical, deductive, divergent, dynamic, emotional, inductive, intuitive, lateral, linear, logical, rational, scientific, static, strategical, tactical, and vertical ways of thinking. However, most of those methods are haphazard, ill-defined, and poorly understood. Furthermore, conventional thinking is incomplete because it ignores the exhaustive possibilities provided by the mind, sensory reality, and their interaction. It is also unsystematic because it lacks an adequate theory and model for the mind, which should justify and integrate those cognitive methods. Conventional thinking is a lose collection of cognitive methods, rather than a coherent cognitive system. Therefore, conventional thinking cannot be taught as a subject in the educational system.

The educational system is a collective that primarily aims to teach people how to fit into the collective. The strength of that collective has gained momentum at the cost of its flexibility. The influence of individual teachers on the direction and quality of the educational system has eroded in favour of economic, ideological, and political stakeholders. Furthermore, the educational system has no adequate method to teach students an exhaustive way of thinking. Therefore, individual teachers cannot be blamed for any failure of the educational system. They can only teach the way of conventional thinking that they have learned themselves. As a result, the educational system is spreading humanity's failing way of thinking as a computer virus. Therefore, the educational system is responsible for creating the reality we live in with all its wonders and brutality.

Some brave teachers argue that they prefer cooperation and teamwork, rather than winning and competition. As the saying goes—*There is no I in team.* However—*There are two I's in winning.* Ironically, education itself is about winning the educational competition, because the grade of each student is evaluated in comparison to the grades of all the other students. Often, the individual grade is even scaled or re-graded to force a national normal distribution for comparison. Furthermore, the real measure of education is revealed during the exams, where teamwork and co-operation are suddenly labelled as 'cheating'. During the most crucial part of education, friendly co-operation is replaced by unfriendly competition. Whatever the grading system, students with low grades are removed from the educational system, while students with higher grades are prepared for the important positions in society. Only the educated will obtain a reasonable living and only the best of them will enjoy the privileges rewarded by the higher levels of society to themselves.

The grading of students by the educational system fosters competition and, therefore, winning is paramount for being successful within the educational system. Although winning and competition might be scorned by some teachers, the educational system as an entity protects the situation with groupthink and cognitive dissonance. As a result, the educational system might select effectively the winners, but it does not maximize the cognitive abilities of the students. The students are conditioned to maximize the probability of winning at the cost of finding the truth. Winning spurious arguments became more important than finding the truth. Debates became arguments for argument's sake. As a result, students might win all their arguments, but they cannot find the truth. Winning is paramount and, therefore, conventional thinking is conflict oriented, which fosters control, force, aggression, enemies, and win-lose strategies. Conventional thinking has become a devastating and self-protecting cognitive virus that destroys the infected individuals and collectives.

Conventional Thinking

Conventional thinking is an incomplete and unsystematic way of thinking that maximizes the probability of winning by applying the way of pseudo-rational thinking that is propagated by the educational system. Conventional thinking aims to maximize the probability of winning competitions and, therefore, it is conflict oriented, which fosters control, force, aggression, enemies, and win-lose strategies.

WEAKNESSES VERSUS STRENGTHS

Nemonik thinkers aim to maximize the probability of success. On the other hand, conventional thinkers are conditioned by the educational system to maximize the probability to win. This apparently small difference has huge implications for the quality of thinking. Conventional thinkers are more likely to fail, because their minds are SCARRED, which is an acronym representing the seven scars or weaknesses of conventional thinking. On the other hand, nemonik thinkers turn those seven weaknesses into strengths.

S.C.A.R.R.E.D

1. **S**tatic, rather than Dynamic thinking.
2. **C**riticizing, rather than Critical thinking.
3. **A**nswering, rather than Questioning.
4. **R**ationalizing, rather than Rational thinking.
5. **R**ighteous, rather than Collective thinking.
6. **E**ducated, rather than Wise.
7. **D**etached, rather than Compassionate.

Static versus Dynamic thinking

Static thinking is a rigid and biased way of thinking that considers only preselected nemoniks and applies those independent of the actual situation. On the other hand, dynamic thinking is a flexible and unbiased way of thinking that considers all seventeen nemoniks equally and applies the ones that fit the actual situation.

The success of the Industrial, Biotech, and Informational Revolutions biased conventional thinkers towards pseudo-rational thinking, which inhibits the application of affectorial thinking. They might be temporarily successful when a static situation demands rational thinking. However, reality is dynamic and the only constant is change. Conventional thinkers will fail when the situation changes and demands ideas, emotional understanding, and a reliance on intuitions and gut-feelings.

The prime aim of conventional thinking is maximizing the probability of winning competitions. However, the rewards of winning will reinforce the repetition of the applied nemoniks, while the pain inflicted by losing will reinforce the avoidance of the applied nemoniks. Hence, the focus on winning fosters a bias towards particular nemoniks. This amplifies the static characteristic of conventional thinking. In order to keep winning, conventional thinkers have to adjust disadvantageous situations to their preselected nemoniks. Therefore, conventional thinking is conflict-oriented, which fosters aggression, enemies, and win-lose strategies.

The prime aim of nemonik thinking is maximizing the probability of success, rather than winning competitions. *Success is to obtain what you seek and escape what you suffer (Lao Zi).* For nemonik thinkers, there are no productive or counterproductive nemoniks. The only constant in the sensory reality is change. Hence, a nemonik that fits perfectly one situation might fail utterly when applied to another situation. Hence, the value of a nemonik is not based on the past experiences with that nemonik. Instead, it depends exclusively on its suitability for the actual situation. The application could be wrong, but the nemonik never is. Therefore, nemonik thinkers remain dynamic in a dynamic sensory reality.

Lao Zi points out—*Competent strategists have no strategy.* In accord, nemonik thinkers use the seventeen nemoniks to create a strategy on the spot to fit the actual situation. They keep adjusting their way of thinking continuously to changes in the situation. In the same way as sailors set their sails to the changing wind. They go with the flow, but they keep their eye on their destiny. The resulting unpredictability is another strength of nemonik thinkers. Furthermore, nemonik thinkers are goal oriented. They adjust to the situation and succeed without control, effort, and force. Therefore, they foster freedom, alignment, compassion, allies, and win-win strategies.

Critics could argue that a system of seventeen nemoniks is too reductionist and mechanical to be dynamic. They might even object that it would create cognitive clones. However, consider the eight notes of music. Those few notes can create an infinite number of melodies. I have never heard of a musician running out of notes. With eight simple keys, the musician controls the hidden electronic complexity of the keyboard. The same is true for nemonik thinking. Just consider nemonik thinking to be a mental keyboard with seventeen keys. Playing that instrument will prompt your complex mind to create an infinite repertoire of smart strategies that will maximize your success.

> Conventional thinking is a static way of thinking that has to control the situation in order to fit that way of thinking. Therefore, conventional thinkers are conflict oriented, which fosters control, force, aggression, enemies, and win-lose strategies. On the other hand, nemonik thinking is a dynamic way of thinking that changes itself in order to fit the actual situation. Therefore, nemonik thinkers are goal oriented, which fosters freedom, alignment, compassion, allies, and win-win strategies.

Criticizing versus Critical thinking

Critical thinking is a part of rational thinking that submits descriptions of reality to reason and logic in order to find the truth. On the other hand, criticizing is a corrupted version of critical thinking that challenges descriptions of reality in order to win debates.

Socrates (470-399 BC) was a Greek philosopher, sculptor, and soldier from Athens who was the teacher of Plato. By emphasizing rational arguments and general definitions, he laid the foundation for rational thinking. Furthermore, he developed critical thinking. However, he did not criticize other people, but asked them critical questions in order to discover the truth e.g.—*What is justice?*

The prime aim of conventional thinking is maximizing the probability of winning and, therefore, it has corrupted Socrates' way of critical thinking. In order to win debates, conventional thinkers apply aggressive forms of criticism to discredit and berate their opponents. They are only silent in order to prepare their poisonous rebuttals. Conventional thinkers focus on the weaknesses and threats associated with the opposing arguments, rather than on the strengths and opportunities provided by those arguments. Hence, they block their own progress by criticizing the argument of their opponent, without obtaining any insight about the advantages of that argument.

For conventional thinkers, winning the argument is paramount and, therefore, they tend to ignore the truth. This counterproductive approach is evident in the crippling debating contests and moot arguments fostered by the educational system. Truth and progress are lost in an idiotic search for popularity and righteousness.

Lawyers win their cases by criticizing the prosecutors. Whether the accused has committed the crime is almost unimportant in the judiciary system—it is about winning or losing the case. Lawyers who cannot criticize their opponents will lose their cases, have no clients, and cede to be lawyers. Politicians win their elections by criticizing their political opponents. The truth of their criticism is also unimportant as long as their statements cannot be disproved during the election period. Politicians who cannot criticize their opponents will have no followers and, therefore, cannot obtain and maintain office. The most eloquent critic will win the debate. However, that winner might still fail, because the loser might have defended the truth. In that case, neither of them will maximize their success. Furthermore, criticizing is conflict oriented, which fosters control, force, aggression, enemies, and win-lose strategies.

In accord with Hegel's dialectic, knowledge develops as a cyclic process that moves each turn closer towards the ultimate truth. His dialectic is demonstrated by the progress of knowledge about the essence of light.

Sir Isaac Newton (1642-1727) was a British mathematician and physicists who described in his book *Principia* the basic laws of nature. He proposed that light was like a stream of tiny particles flying through space like cannonballs.[149] This thesis was in accord with his law of motion.[150] In contrast, Thomas Young (1773-1829) conducted the famous double-split experiment that supported the widely accepted antithesis that light moves through space like a wave.[151] Both arguments were correct and, therefore, the evidence that light consist of particles could not reject the evidence that light consist of waves and vice versa. As a result, both groups got stuck in criticizing each other. That criticism maintained a counterproductive debate that inhibited scientific progress for decades. A wise friend of mine said once—*If you are in a hole, then stop digging!*

In 1905, Albert Einstein accepted Thomas Young's antithesis, but returned also to Newton's thesis that light manifests itself as a stream of particles.[152] In Hegelian terminology, Einstein synthesized Newton's thesis with Young's antithesis. He proposed that light moves through space and transparent matter both as a particle and a wave.

Hegel's dialectic implies that knowledge is a process, rather than a state. In accord, reality shows that the volume of scientific research accelerates daily and, therefore, the journey is not finished. As long as Hegel's dialectic continues, we cannot claim to know the truth. The rational truth is a static belief in a specific description of reality. We are on a journey and what we know is the last step on that journey, rather than the destiny. Einstein's synthesis concerning the essence of light might be just another thesis awaiting the next antithesis.

The practical question is—*How do we accelerate our thinking?* Hegel's dialectic is a passive description, rather than a method. In contrast, the nemonik accelerator is a cognitive method that will accelerate actively the progress of knowledge.

If everyone agrees with a thesis, then progress in that area will stop. In such situations, cognitive dissonance and groupthink maintain the status quo. Persistent dissidents are often silenced with the obstructive statement—*Let us agree to disagree!* As a result, Newton's thesis that light consists of particles stood unchallenged for about two hundred years. In contrast, nemonik thinkers will foster disagreement during such a state of agreement. They will search for the antithesis. They will use their creative mindmodes to challenge the status quo, find weaknesses of the thesis, provide alternatives, put things upside down, and play the Devil's Advocate.

If advocates of a thesis and antithesis keep criticizing each other, then progress in that area will stop again. Therefore, nemonik thinkers will search for the inevitable synthesis. In accord with the nemonik accelerator, they will foster agreement during such a state of disagreement. During disagreements, they will use their creative mindmodes to find compatibilities, holistic features, patterns, relationships, similarities, and the strengths of both the thesis and antithesis.

If you want to maximize your success, rather than winning debates, then it is in your interest to accelerate your thinking. The nemonik accelerator is a cognitive method that increases the speed of your thinking by fostering agreement during disagreement, while fostering disagreement during agreement. Even if you believe that a thesis is true, your only way forward is finding the antithesis. Do not wait until someone else comes along with a valid antithesis. On the other hand, if you are facing both a thesis and an antithesis, then your only way forward is merging them into a synthesis. Again, do not wait for someone else to prove you wrong by providing a synthesis.

Nemonik thinkers are critical thinkers. They focus on finding the truth, rather than winning debates. They focus as much on their own argument as on the opposing argument. They evaluate impartially the strength, weaknesses, opportunities, and threats of both arguments. Nemonik thinkers are goal-oriented and, therefore, they foster freedom, alignment, compassion, allies, and win-win strategies.

> The competition within the educational system forces conventional thinkers to maximize the probability of winning by criticizing others. Therefore, conventional thinkers are conflict oriented, which fosters control, force, aggression, enemies, and win-lose strategies. On the other hand, nemonik thinkers apply critical thinking to maximize the probability of success. Therefore, nemonik thinking is goal oriented, which fosters freedom, alignment, compassion, allies, and win-win strategies.

Answering versus Questioning

It is the prime aim of the educational system to select the right student for the right position in society. Therefore, it has to foster an impartial and effective mass-grading system. In general, the quality of answers is far easier to evaluate than the quality of questions. After all, a fool can ask more questions than hundred sages could answer. Therefore, the quality of the answers has become the prime measure of the educational system. Consequently, students are conditioned as Pavlovian dogs to answer questions, rather than to question the questions.

To ease the grading process, teachers ask often forced-choice or closed-ended questions so that the answer of the student is either right or wrong. To prevent a total mental shut-down of their students; teachers might prompt the memories of their students by providing multiple-choices for the required answers. Nevertheless, that approach still limits the responses of the students. For example, what is your favourite colour—Red, yellow, purple, or blue? Unfortunately, I prefer green! My option is not on the list. Depending on my creativity, I might want to improve the question. However, thinking about the question is a distraction from the required answer, which will not maximize my grade. In addition, the memory prompting associated with multiple-choices erodes the recall abilities of the students. This creates a cognitive weakness, because there are no easy prompts in real life. Even if essay-questions are used, the question itself is still not to be questioned by the student. The educational system should teach students how to think and memorize before uploading them with fast outdating information.

The failure of the educational system to train students adequately in questioning questions continues to the highest level. Only Master and PhD candidates are required to propose and test their own question or hypothesis. That is one question after about two decades of intensive study. Unfortunately, it is in the very creative nature of a genius to question questions. Despite all the lip-service, this heretic approach has been strongly discouraged by the educational system. For example, Albert Einstein was one of the many geniuses who were rejected by the educational system. Not understanding Einstein's questioning way of thinking, his tutor Minkowski called him even a 'lazy dog'. To add insult to injury, this superb thinker was forced to accept a job as a second clerk in a Swiss patent office.

The educational requirement to answer prepared questions, forces the students to memorize the provided information, rather than to think about that information. Hence, conventional thinkers are conditioned to foster their memory at the cost of their thinking. They are conditioned to recall information without processing. This unintended inhibition of thinking is counterproductive for the individual and the collective. Furthermore, the competition within the educational system demands students to maximize the probability of winning even at the cost of the truth. Despite its obvious weaknesses, the system is maintained, because narrowing education to answering prepared questions fosters the effective mass-grading of students.

The educational system forces conventional thinkers to answer questions, rather than questioning questions. However, the right answers might win debates at the cost of success. For example, nowadays, politicians ask scientists what to do about the effects of industrial global warming. Some scientists proclaim that the industrial carbon dioxide emissions have to be lowered. However, that might be indeed the right answer on the wrong question.

Nemonik thinkers maximize the probability of success. Therefore, they question the question, before they answer a question. For example, the 420,000 years of data extracted from the Antarctic ice-core, suggest that the next ice-age is a few thousand years overdue. In addition, the current carbon dioxide level of 400 ppm predicts a temperature of 11.5 °C, while the current global warming is only 1.3 °C.[xi] This thermal gap of 10.2 °C suggests that the next ice-age has already started and decreased the temperature from 11.5 to 1.3 °C. The increase in industrial carbon dioxide emissions might mask the low glacial temperatures.

Removing industrial carbon dioxide emissions during such an ice-age could endanger the survival of humanity. Low carbon dioxide levels in combination with low temperatures would cause a catastrophic reduction in the food supply. That would force billions of people in the colder regions to leave everything behind and move towards the equator. As shown in Europe, we cannot even cope with two million Syrian refuges. Hence, questioning the question is often more important than answering that question. The politicians might have to ask the scientists what to do about global cooling. Industrial global warming could be the solution for natural global cooling.[153]

Nemonik thinking is not a choice between answering questions and questioning questions. Nemonik thinkers question

---

[xi] Parts per million (ppm). Degrees Celsius (°C).

the questions before trying to answer any questions. Asking questions might open closed minds. Nevertheless, questions are not always appreciated by the establishment. Socrates became famous for his questioning approach, but he was still executed by his government for his daring questions.

> The mass-grading of the educational system conditions conventional thinkers to answer prepared questions. Therefore, such thinkers are prone to find the right answers on the wrong questions. On the other hand, nemonik thinkers question the question before they answer any question. Therefore, nemonik thinkers are more likely to find the right answers on the right questions.

Rationalizing versus Rational thinking

Rationalizing is a corrupted version of rational thinking that provides pseudo-rational justifications to defend a previously made conclusion. In rationalization, facts are used to defend the conclusion, while in rational thinking those facts are used to test the conclusion.

Aristotle developed the validity rules for logic that form the basis for rational thinking. Those rules lead our thinking from true facts to true conclusions about reality. In turn, those conclusions become the new facts and so on. Rational thinking initiated amazing phenomena such as the Renaissance and the Industrial, Biotech, and Informational Revolutions. Nevertheless, people had to compete with each other in that new reality to obtain an advantageous position. In their constant struggle to the top, students, warriors, businesspersons, lawyers, politicians, etc. were conditioned to win competitions. Ultimately, winning debates became more important than discovering the truth. As a result, conventional thinking corrupted rational thinking into rationalizing.

Conventional thinkers maximize the probability of winning debates by turning rational thinking into rationalizing. They determine first the conclusion and then search for statements supporting that conclusion. Ultimately, the rationalization of personal opinions and beliefs replaces the truth obtained with rational thinking. Similar to criticism, rationalization nurtures debating classes and moot arguments, which is wasting precious resources on arguments for argument's sake. Conventional thinking fosters rationalizations that are conflict-oriented, which fosters control, force, aggression, enemies, and win-lose strategies.

Libraries are filled with rejected information that was once considered the eternal truth. Taking ownership of such information fosters the defence of outdated information. For nemonik thinkers, each thesis, antithesis, or synthesis is only one of the many steps towards the elusive truth. Nemonik thinkers focus on their success and, therefore, they reject ownership of any thesis, antithesis, or synthesis. Rationalizing opinions for the sake of winning debates, decreases the probability of your success. Therefore, nemonik thinkers apply rational thinking to obtain the truth. That goal-oriented approach fosters freedom, alignment, compassion, allies, and win-win strategies.

Conventional thinkers maximize the probability of winning debates by rationalizing their predetermined conclusions. Therefore, such thinkers are conflict oriented, which fosters control, force, aggression, enemies, and win-lose strategies. On the other hand, nemonik thinkers maximize the probability of success by applying rational thinking to discover the truth. Therefore, nemonik thinkers are goal oriented, which fosters freedom, alignment, compassion, allies, and win-win strategies.

Righteous versus Collective thinking

Righteous thinking is a corrupted version of collective thinking that creates rights without obligations for privileged individuals within a collective. Confucius suggested—*Do not do to others, what you do not want others to do to you.* I would like to add—*Do for others, what you want others to do for you.* In accord, collective thinking creates artificial rules to regulate and strengthen the cooperation between the members of a collective.

Students are conditioned to win the educational competition, because the 'losers' will become outcasts in their own society. This concealed threat forces them to win even at the cost of their collective. Therefore, they replace collective thinking with righteous thinking by claiming their collective rights and rejecting their collective obligations. As a result, collective values such as morality, generosity, honesty, honour, and loyalty have been replaced by egocentric values such as entertainment, greed, deceit, materialism, and betrayal. Furthermore, in order to win, the conventional thinkers have to occupy also the moral high ground. Therefore, being looking right has become more important than being right.

Righteous accountants help the rich to evade their taxes; righteous lawyers help criminals to avoid their punishments; righteous business owners feed their greed and righteous politicians struggle for personal power. However, tax evasion, crime, inequality, and rebellion weaken the collective. Hence, righteous thinkers might win within the protection of their collective, but their collective will certainly lose. There is no escape. Righteous thinkers are climbing the mast of the sinking Titanic.

Some might argue that I overstate my case, but look at the millions of refugees on this planet. They include previous accountants, rich people, lawyers, criminals, business owners, and politicians. Each of them might have won every fight within their profession, but they were still not successful. Their lives are destroyed and their loved ones killed, because their urge to win at all cost broke down the collective that protected them. To maximize the probability of winning, conventional thinkers tend to apply righteous thinking. However, that weakens their collective by claiming rights without accepting obligations. Therefore, conventional thinkers are conflict oriented, which fosters control, force, aggression, enemies, and win-lose strategies.

Some African tribes have developed the concept of *'Ubuntu'*, which means—*I am, because we are.* It emphasizes that no individual can survive without the support of a strong collective. In accord, nemonik thinkers apply collective thinking, rather than righteous thinking. To maximize the probability of success, they strengthen their collective by balancing individual rights and obligations. The aim to maintain that balance is goal-oriented goal oriented and, therefore, nemonik thinkers foster freedom, alignment, compassion, allies, and win-win strategies.

> Conventional thinkers use righteous thinking to maximize the probability of winning by creating individual rights without obligations. Therefore, such thinkers are conflict oriented, which fosters control, force, aggression, enemies, and win-lose strategies. On the other hand, nemonik thinkers use collective thinking to maximize the probability of success by balancing the individual rights with obligations. Therefore, nemonik thinkers are goal oriented, which fosters freedom, alignment, compassion, allies, and win-win strategies.

Educated versus Wise

Education is a mental process that transfers systematically detailed knowledge and skills from a teacher to a student. Hence, an educated person is in the possession of knowledge. In contrast, wisdom is the productive application of knowledge to the actual situation. For example, knowledge is remembering how to make a fire. Wisdom is the cognitive ability to warm your house with a fire without burning it down. Wisdom is our mental resonance with nature. A person could have knowledge without wisdom. However, no one could have wisdom without knowledge. Such wisdom is an echo of pompous words without any meaning.

As mentioned previously, it is the prime aim of the educational system to prepare the right student for the right position. Therefore, the educational system has to mass-grade its students. However, wisdom is notoriously difficult to evaluate. Therefore, the recall ability of the students is the prime measure of their mental abilities. As a result, the educational system conditions conventional thinkers to focus on retaining detailed knowledge at the cost of acquiring holistic wisdom.

Although a magician is able to distort the perception of the sensory reality, the spectators do not believe their own senses. The 'facts' are there, and nevertheless, those facts are not believed. Instead, the mind wonders—*How did he do it?* Conventional thinkers foster rational knowledge and inhibit affectorial beliefs. However, the difference between knowledge and belief is ambiguous. Ultimately, even the most reliable and valid knowledge requires an affectorial believe in that knowledge in order to be perceived as true.

Education lacks a systematic way of thinking and an adequate model of the mind that could be used to teach students how to think. Therefore, the emphasis of the educational system has been on transferring knowledge, rather than on processing knowledge. Conventional thinkers emphasize memorizing, rather than thinking. Therefore, they are biased towards knowing, rather than wisdom. Unfortunately, reality shows that the resulting way of conventional thinking is failing. On the other hand, it is difficult to think without having knowledge stored in your memory. There would be nothing to think about. Therefore, nemonik thinkers foster equally memorizing and thinking.

Nemonik thinkers foster wisdom by maximizing the probability of success, rather than winning competitions. Hence, they focus on the long-term effects, limitations, and repercussions of applying their knowledge. Nemonik thinkers inhibit blind-spots by evaluating all aspects of the mind, sensory reality, and their interaction. Furthermore, nemonik thinkers foster wisdom, because they rely on rational facts, logic, reason, and rules, but also on affectorial intuitions, emotions, creativity, and intuition. They use all their holistic mindpower to maximize their success.

Nemonik thinkers foster wisdom because they inhibit the SCARRED weaknesses of conventional thinkers. The nemonik accelerator fosters wisdom because it inhibits stagnation, closed mindedness, and counterproductive debates. Nemonik thinkers foster wisdom, because they question the questions and, therefore, they focus on the underlying problems. Nemonik thinkers foster wisdom because they are goal oriented, rather than conflict oriented. Nemonik thinkers foster wisdom by focusing on the truth, rather than on winning counterproductive debates and rationalizations. Nemonik thinkers create and maintain strong collectives—they build bridges, rather than fences. Hence, their wisdom fosters freedom, alignment, compassion, allies, and win-win strategies.

> The competitive mass-grading of the educational system is conditioning conventional thinkers to memorize knowledge at the cost of obtaining wisdom. On the other hand, nemonik thinking fosters wisdom because it includes all the aspects of thinking and is dynamic in the dynamic sensory reality.

Detached versus Compassionate

Detachment is the rationalized impartiality in regard to other people that fosters competitive behaviour in order to maximize the probability of winning. On the other hand, compassion is the affectorial sympathy for other people that inhibits competitive behaviour in order to maximize the probability of success.

The recent success of reason and logic in science and technology has biased conventional thinkers towards rational thinking. By definition, rational thinking fosters objectivity and inhibits affecters such as compassion. In addition, the educational system has conditioned them to maximize their probability of winning, which turns rational thinking into pseudo-rational thinking. As a result, conventional thinkers detach themselves from the problems of their collectives, including family, friends, colleagues, and allies.

The detachment of conventional thinkers fosters a ruthless approach in regard to the treatment of other people. In order to soothe their conscience and stay on the moral high ground, conventional thinkers rationalize their cold-hearted detachment by blaming their victims. Many rich people detach themselves from the poor by blaming the victims for their poverty. They proclaim—*They are just lazy! It is just business! They do not want any help!* Accountants detach themselves from the taxpayers by pointing out that they are just doing their job and act within the law. Criminals detach themselves from their victims by saying—*It is nothing personal. We live in a world where dogs eat dogs.* Their lawyers detach themselves from the victims by arguing—*Each criminal has the right of a fair trial.* Conventional thinkers are detached, rather than compassionate. That detachment is conflict oriented, which fosters control, force, aggression, enemies, and win-lose strategies.

Independent of the situation, conventional thinkers foster detachment and inhibit compassion in order to maximize the probability of winning. On the other hand, dependent on the situation, nemonik thinkers foster either detachment or compassion in order to maximize the probability of success.

The most precious things in life are associated with the affectorial mindmode, rather than with the rational one. Beauty, belief, love, friendship, comradery, belonging, wisdom, talent, creativity, and intuition, cannot be measured with logic and reason. The detachment associated with conventional thinking is likely to destroy those affectorial treasures.

Compassion is the basic force that creates and maintains a collective. The effect of the collective on the individual cannot be underestimated—*I am, because we are!* History has shown repeatedly that people will sacrifice their lives out of compassion for their collective. Any individual without a strong and supportive collective is doomed to fail. Nemonik thinkers are no do-gooders. They strive to develop genuine compassion for their own sake. Compassion will help them to maximize their probability of success. As their compassion is for their own sake, it will last. Like all karma, compassion returns compassion.

> The aim of conventional thinkers is to maximize their probability of winning, which requires pseudo-rational thinking. Therefore, they are detached, which fosters conflict orientation, control, force, aggression, enemies, and win-lose strategies. On the other hand, the aim of nemonik thinkers is to maximize their success, which requires the unbiased use of rational and affectorial thinking. Therefore, they are compassionate, which fosters goal orientation, freedom, alignment, compassion, allies, and win-win strategies.

THE COGNITIVE CS7-VIRUS

A virus is a small entity that lives in a host and is concealed, self-replicating, and self-protective. A benign virus lives in symbiosis within its host, while a malignant virus destroys its host. In 1889, Martinus Beijerink discovered the first biological virus. Since then, scientists have discovered about 5,000 biological viruses including AIDS, Ebola, Influenza, and Zika. Furthermore, in 1971, Bob Thomas wrote the first computer virus, which he called the 'Creeper system'. To date, a billion dollar industry is needed to protect our artificial intelligence against malignant computer viruses. Herewith, I introduce the first malignant cognitive virus called 'CS7'. This virus is more devastating than any biological or computer virus known to date.

CS7 is a cognitive, self-protective, malignant, contagious, self-replicating, and epidemical virus that creates and maintains humanity's failing way of conventional thinking. CS stands for 'Cognitive Scars', while the number 7 refers to the seven cognitive scars that create and maintain conventional thinking. Those seven scars are represented by the previously explained acronym SCARRED. In accord, conventional thinkers are biased towards—staticism, criticism, answering, rationalization, righteousness, education, and detachment.

CS7 is a cognitive virus because it affects the individual and collective ways of thinking. Furthermore, we use our infected natural intelligence to create artificial intelligence. Therefore, CS7 infects inevitably also our artificial intelligence. Consequently, the hope that artificial intelligence will solve our problems is entirely misplaced. More likely, computers will accelerate and magnify our problems—*Rubbish in, more rubbish out.* We have to improve our thinking, before we could even hope to design smarter computers.

The AIDS-virus attacks the immune system of the body. Similarly, the CS7-virus attacks the immune system of the mind. The mental immune system protects the information that is already accepted by the mind as correct. However, that protection becomes malignant when the mind protects incorrect information. In that case, the subconscious reactive mindmode releases affecters to the conscious that create cognitive dissonance. Cognitive dissonance is an individual mental process rejecting correct information in order to protect the incorrect information that is already accepted by the subconscious of that individual as true. The collective equivalent of cognitive dissonance is called groupthink. Groupthink is a collective mental process rejecting correct information in order to protect incorrect information that is already accepted by the collective as true. Cognitive dissonance and groupthink are expressed as aggression, agreeing to disagree, changing the topic, excessive talking, interrupting, passive silence, passive aggression, shouting, threats, and outright violence.

The immune system of the body does not recognize malignant cancer cells as a threat. Similarly, the immune system of the mind does not recognize the malignant CS7-virus as a threat. The subconscious reactive mindmode is the location of the CS7 infection and, therefore, the conscious will always receive affecters that support CS7. As a result, any outside attempt to improve the way of conventional thinking is seen as a threat by the beholders. They close their minds to reality and believe that they are correct despite clear evidence to the contrary. Furthermore, the peer pressure of groupthink will force deviant thinkers to conform to the failed collective way of conventional thinking. Hence, the CS7-virus protects itself with cognitive dissonance and groupthink.

Make no mistake; although CS7 is almost impossible to detect by your conscious, it is a malignant and deadly virus. It creates and maintains humanity's failing way of conventional thinking. As a result, the next generation is facing a legacy of overpopulation, dwindling resources, pollution, climate change, nuclear warfare, empty oceans, deforestation, growing deserts, famine, etc. CS7 threatens the survival of our entire species including you and your collectives. In addition, the side effects of CS7 annihilate other species and destroy the eco-system of our planet. Under such conditions, aiming to maximize the probability of winning is unproductive. It is like climbing the mast of the sinking Titanic. Even if you could escape to another planet, then you would still fail. You are carrying the CS7-virus and, therefore, you would recreate the same problems on that new planet. The only effective antidote to CS7 is a smarter way of thinking that aims to maximize the probability of success, rather than winning.

The CS7-virus is highly contagious, because it is self-replicating. It spreads through any direct or indirect cognitive contact between people. In addition, the global educational system propagates this virus vigorously by conditioning students to maximize the probability of winning at the cost of maximizing the probability of success. The reinforcement that is used for that conditioning is extremely strong. Only students indoctrinated with CS7 are allowed to succeed. As a reward, they receive the power, status, and wealth of the collective. They become the new collective gate-keepers for CS7. Hence, the level of internalization of the virus determines the quality and duration of one's life.

Right now, the spread of the CS7-virus is of epidemical proportions. Due to the educational system, that virus has already infected all economical, educational, industrial, military, political, scientific, and social strata of the global collective. This notion is supported by humanity's increasing list of unsolved global problems.

The incubation period of a virus is the time between the initial exposure to that virus and the first appearance of its symptoms. The incubation period of the CS7-virus equals the duration required for the educational indoctrination of conventional thinking. Hence, I propose the hypothesis that the malignant strength of CS7 is positively correlated to the duration of one's education. Therefore, the infection is most malignant in the top of our collectives.

The origin of the CS7-virus lies firmly in the educational system. Despite all the red herrings, winning the educational competition is paramount for the quality and quantity of one's life. The educational system conditions students with pass/fail grades to win competitions. Therefore, it fosters by default conventional thinking, which comprises corrupted versions of critical, rational, and collective thinking. However, conventional thinking inhibits the truth and, therefore, it fails and creates the malignant cognitive virus CS7. In turn, that virus consolidates conventional thinking with cognitive dissonance and groupthink. The inhibition of the truth has made deceit a lucrative profession. It provides wealth and power for spin-doctors, campaign managers, news media, political lobbyists, and advertising and public relations agencies. They turn loyalty, honesty, and compassion into betrayal, deception, detachment, arrogance, and greed. As a result of their manipulative smoke and mirrors, humanity is deceived to the point of self-destruction. To date, the only known antidote to the malignant cognitive CS7-virus is nemonik thinking.

SCARRED

The main weaknesses of conventional thinking are static thinking, criticizing, answering, rationalizing, righteousness, education, and detachment. The main strengths of nemonik thinking are dynamic thinking, critical thinking, questioning, rational thinking, collective thinking, wisdom, and compassion.

YOUR DECISION

It is in your interest to become the best thinker you can be. Volunteer to help yourself! Going through the motions of nemonik thinking is like weight lifting—it creates mental muscles. When you are experienced enough, then you will not think about nemonik thinking anymore. It is the same as driving a car. If you are an experienced driver, then you do not think consciously about driving. You just do it! Hence, it is in your advantage to practise nemonik thinking until your reactive mindmode has created a mindset for it. That mindset will foster your ability to think on your feet inhibiting stress and panic. Think smarter with nemonik thinking. Whatever you seek or try to escape, nemonik thinking will maximize your success. All it takes is 17 words!

Perfection

Reality is dynamic and, therefore, perfection has to be dynamic. One moment a phenomenon is perfect and the next it is imperfect because the situation has changed. Perfection is the ability to adjust to the changes in reality. Perfection is a process, rather than a state. In accord, the perfect way of nemonik thinking is the one that fits the actual situation. In accord, nemonik thinking is a step forward but it is not the end of our cognitive journey. Therefore, you are invited to develop the antithesis of nemonik thinking. In that way, our thinking will remain perfect.

Notes

APPENDICES

INDEX

BIBLIOGRAPHY

Botting, S. (2015, March Friday 6). A question of memory. *Othago Daily Times*, 17.

Branson Sir, R. (1999). *Losing my Virginity: The Autobiography.* Australia: Random House Australia.

Confucius. (1979). *The Analects.* (B. Radice, Ed., & D. C. Lau, Trans.) Middlesex, England: Penguin Books.

de Bono, E. (1970). *Lateral Thinking.* New York, USA: Harper & Row, Publishers.

Duka, P. (1897). *The Sorcerer's Apprentice (Orchestral Scherzo).*

Foot, I. C. (Ed.). (1995). *The Oxford Companion to the Second World War.* Oxford: Oxford University Press.

FungYulan. (1983). *A History of Chinese Philosophy.* (D. Bodde, Trans.) USA: Princeton University Press.

Gracián, B. (1993). *The Art of Worldly Wisdom by Baltasar Gracián.* (C. Mauer, Trans.) London: Mandarin Paperbacks.

Gracian, B. (1994). *The Art of Worldly Wisdom.* (C. Maurer, Trans.) William Heinemann Ltd.

Gribben, J. (1999). *Get a Grip on New Physics.* London, UK: Weidenfield and Nicolson.

Hawking, S. (1998). *A Brief History of Time.* Great Britain: Bantam Press.

Hoffmann, Y. (1977). *The Sound of the One Hand.* Granada Publishing Limited.

Kaku, M. (1994). *Hyperspace.* New York: Oxford University Press, Inc.

Lorenz, E. (1963). Deterministic nonperiodic flow. *Journal of Atmospheric Sciences, 20*, 130-141.

Mencius. (1970). *The Works of Mencius.* (J. Legge, Trans.) New York: Dover Publications Inc.

Newton Sir, I. (1687). *Philosophiae Naturalis Principia Mathematica (The Mathematical Principles of Natural Philosophy).*

Oxford Dictionary of Psychology. (2003). Oxford: Oxford University Press.

Sawyer, R. D. (1993). *The Seven Military Classics of Ancient China.* (R. D. Sawyer, Trans.) Summertown, Oxford: Westview Press.

Schade, A. (1995). *Quantitative measures and models for the assessment of thermal biofeedback as a specific treatment for migraine and non-organic headache.* New Zealand: The University of Auckland.

Schade, A. (2015). bioPAD: Nemonik Thinking (PowerPoint). Dunedin: nemonik-thinking.org.

Schade, A. (2016). *Dictionary Nemonik Thinking.* nemonik-thinking.org.

Schade, A. (2016). *Global Warming is the Solution.* nemonik-thinking.org.

Schade, A. (2016). *Glossary Nemonik Thinking.* nemonik-thinking.org.

Schade, A. (planned 2017). *Baltasar Gracián's Wisdom for Nemonik Thinkers.* nemonik-thinking.org.

Schade, A. (planned 2017). *Lao Zi's Dao De Jing.* nemonik-thinking.org.

Schade, A. (planned 2017). *Sun Zi's The Art of War.* nemonik-thinking.org.

Schade, A. (planned 2017). *The Unreal Reality.* nemonik-thinking.org.

Spencer, H. (1930). *In Chalmers Mitchell, Sir P., Materialism and Vitalism in Biology. The Herbert Spencer lecture, 1930, p. 5.* Claredon Press.

Suzuki, D. (1956). *Zen Buddhism.* (W. Barret, Ed.) USA: Doubleday Anchor Books.

LIST OF TABLES

GLOSSARY

#

80/20 rule—in 20% of the time required doing a perfect job; people are able to complete 80% of that job to a reasonable standard.

A

Abnormal—collective judgement that a person's internal reality is outside the collectively accepted perception of the sensory reality.

Accept—perceptual nemonik that prompts the mind to accept the incoming information as a true description of the sensory reality.

Accumulate—material nemonik that prompts the mind to increase the amount of matter that is under control.

Act—temporal nemonik that prompts the mind to change or move matter in space and time.

Advance—spatial nemonik that prompts the mind to decrease the distance to the goal.

Affecters—mental signals that are generated by subconscious affectorial thinking, which influence the conscious without explaining the underlying subconscious processes.

Affectorial bias—consistent preference for affectorial thinking that is independent of the situation in the sensory reality.

Affectorial thinking—subconscious part of nemonik thinking that deals with the unpredictable chaos of reality by generating affecters that influence the conscious.

Algorithm—set of rules comprising a computational procedure, which follows a definite path to the single solution of a problem.

Analects—book comprising the ideas of Confucius, which were compiled by his students after his death.

Antithesis—tested description of reality that contradicts a thesis.

Aphorisms—folk wisdoms, heuristics, rules of thumb, truisms, clichés, definitions, mottos, and proverbs.

Aristotle (384-322 BC)—Greek philosopher who developed the validity rules for reason, which form the basis for rational thinking.

Artificial—refers to that part of the sensory reality that is manmade.

Artificial facts—changeable facts that are only true within a particular collective because they are based on collective decisions.

Artificial knowledge—knowledge about the artificial rules of a collective.

Artificial rules—descriptions of the changeable cause-effect relationships that are only true within a particular collective, because they are based on decisions of that collective.

Association—spontaneous mental jump from one concept to another related concept that is stored in the memory.

Auto-balance—dynamic balance between the state of the mind and the state of the body, which moves on a continuum ranging from tension to relaxation.

B

Behaviour—the observable physical activity of an organism.

Belief—acceptance of an untestable description of reality.

Bilateral thinking—nemonik thinking incorporates two complementary ways of thinking in order to cope with the order and chaos of the perceived dual reality. In accord, the conscious generates rational thinking to deal with the perceived order of reality, while the larger subconscious generates affectorial thinking to deal with the perceived chaos of reality.

Biofeedback—learning process to control consciously an auditory or optical feedback signal that represents a subconsciously regulated physical process.

Blitzkrieg—coordinated high-speed military advance that fosters momentum, internal assistance, bypasses obstacles, and concentrates on the ultimate goal. This strategy was designed by Heinz Wilhelm Guderian.

Body—material part of a person, which is composed of organic cells and substances that are organised into a living system.

Brainstorming—non-critical group technique that creates random ideas by fostering a silent mind, free expression, disorganization, and association, while inhibiting rational thinking.

Brainware—set of self-organizing organic components and processes that support the mindware. In computer terminology, brainware could be compared to the hardware of a computer.

Butterfly effect—associated with Lorenz's *Chaos Theory.* Although the universe might be a deterministic system, small differences in the initial conditions cause unpredictable outcomes or chaos.

C

Chaos or disorder – part of the external reality that cannot be subjected to reason. It is associated with incomprehensibility, belief, predictability, unrecognizability, etc. The mind developed subconscious affectorial thinking to deal with the chaos of reality. Antonym—Order.

Cognitive dissonance—individual mental process rejecting correct information in order to protect the incorrect information that is already accepted by the subconscious of that individual as true. Cognitive dissonance can be expressed by aggression, agreeing to disagree, changing the topic, excessive talking, interrupting, passive silence, passive aggression, shouting, and violence.

Cognitive irrelevance—new information does not fit into the information that we have already stored in our memory.

Cognitive relevance—new information fits into the information that we have already stored in our memory.

Collective—(1) mental nemonik referring to the collective mindmode. (2) An organized group of people with a common goal such as a family, business, tribe, nation, or the entire human race. (3) A description of the external reality that depends on the beliefs and perceptions of a particular group of people.

Collective mindmode—way of rational thinking that generates artificial rules, which determine the rights and obligations of individuals within a collective and makes their behaviours predictable.

Collective specialists—operate where artificial rules are crucial such as in accountancy, bureaucracy, judiciary, and government.

Compassion (Chinese *ci*)—affectorial sympathy for other people that inhibits competitive behaviour in order to maximize the probability of success. Compassion is one of Lao Zi's three treasures.

Computer programmer—See Programmer.

Conceal—projectional nemonik that prompts the mind to project false information to the sensory reality.

Concentration—intentional mental process that fosters conscious dominance by focusing consciously on a particular aspect of the sensory reality in order to inhibit unintentional conscious thoughts. Opposite—Relaxation. See Meditation, Nemonik meditation.

Confucius, Kung Ciu, or Kung Chung-ni (551-479 BC)—Chinese philosopher who was one of the first to address the problems concerning the artificial rules of the collectives. He was a contemporary of Lao Zi. However, Lao Zi's philosophy diametrically opposes the ideas of Confucius. Confucius elaborated on what Lao Zi calls The Way of People (Chinese *De*). Lao Zi pointed out that The Way of Nature (Chinese *Dao*) is always superior to The Way of the People. After Confucius' death, his students compiled his ideas in a manuscript called: *The Analects.*

Conscious—small part of the mind that is only active when that person is fully awake. The conscious is associated with awareness, concentration, learning, sensory reality, and rational thinking.

Conscious dominance—healthy mental state that is fostered by concentration. During this state, the conscious is active, while the conscious awareness of subconscious activity is inhibited.

Consistent arguments—feature a strong connection between the facts. In the argument (A > B, B > C, therefore A > C), (B is a common factor in the facts A > B and B > C).

Conventional thinking—incomplete and unsystematic way of thinking that maximizes the probability of winning by applying the way of pseudo-rational thinking that is propagated by the educational system.

Convergent thinking—way of thinking that aims to provide the only correct answer on a specific question. The term convergent thinking was coined by Joy Paul Guilford.

Copernicus, Nicolaus (1473-1543)—Polish astronomer who introduced the idea that the Earth orbits the Sun.

Creative—(1) mental nemonik that refers to the creative mindmode. (2) A new description of reality.

Creative affecters—new descriptions of the chaos of reality, which are generated by the creative mindmode. They include discoveries, fantasies, ideas, innovations, insights, inspirations, inventions, novelties, etc.

Creative mindmode—way of affectorial thinking that deals with the unknown or inexperienced aspects of reality by generating creative affecters.

Critical thinking—part of rational thinking that submits descriptions of reality to reason and logic in order to find the truth.

Criticizing—corrupted version of critical thinking that challenges descriptions of reality in order to win debates.

CS7-virus—cognitive, self-protective, malignant, contagious, self-replicating, and epidemical virus that creates and maintains humanity's failing way of conventional thinking. CS stands for 'Cognitive Scars', while the number 7 refers to the seven cognitive scars that create and maintain conventional thinking. Those seven scars are represented by the previously explained acronym SCARRED. In accord, conventional thinkers are biased towards—staticism, criticism, answering, rationalization, righteousness, education, and detachment.

D

da Vinci, Leonardo (1452-1519)—Italian Renaissance genius during the period of the High Renaissance. He excelled as an anatomist, architect, botanist, cartographer, engineer, geologist, inventor, mathematician, musician, painter, sculptor, and writer.

Dao De Jing—book written by Lao Zi about two-and-half thousand years ago. *Dao De Jing* means a classic (*Jing*) about the Way of Nature (*Dao*) and the Way of People (*De*). Nowadays, we call the Way of the Nature *Physics*, while the Way of the people has become *Psychology*. Thus, the modern meaning of *Dao De Jing* is: *A Classic about Physics and Psychology*.

de Bono, Edward (1933--)—Maltese consultant, inventor, and physician who introduced lateral thinking in 1970. Lateral thinking is a way of creative thinking that reformulates problems and looks at them from different perspectives in order to find solutions.

Decision-making—the conscious might reason, but the subconscious will decide. The real decisions are made by the subconscious, while the conscious receives the decisions as affecters from the reactive mindmode. After that, the conscious might rationalize the decisions.

Deductive thinking—conscious way of thinking that derives a conclusion from one or more facts. For example, (Fact 1: All men are mortal) (Fact 2: Socrates is a man) (Conclusion: Socrates is mortal). More than two thousand years ago, the Greek philosophers Socrates, Plato, and Aristotle initiated the development of deductive thinking.

Deepening—using mantras to increase semiconscious dominance.

Defragmentation—reorganizing separated information into united information. It is like organizing a random pile of books into a systematic library. After that organization, all the books about a particular topic are stored in the same place.

Delusion - incorrect belief that is maintained in the face of contrasting reason.

Detachment—rationalized impartiality in regard to other people that fosters competitive behaviour in order to maximize the probability of winning.

Detection—process of perceiving sensory signals through the senses.

Determinism—notion that future phenomena are fully determined by their initial conditions.

Devil's advocate—literally an official who puts the case against the beatification or canonization. In daily life, the person who always defends the opposite or antithesis.

Directional expansion—growth of a collective or individual towards a predetermined mission.

Disorder—See Chaos.

Disorganizing or randomizing—process of transforming order into chaos.

Dispose—material nemonik that prompts the mind to decrease the amount matter that is under control.

Divergent thinking—way of creative thinking that aims to provide multiple solutions for a single problem. The term divergent thinking was coined by Joy Paul Guilford.

Dominance window—hypothetical window that determines the mental state by sliding over the mental continuum, which ranges from conscious dominance to subconscious dominance.

Dream awareness—conscious awareness of subconscious dreams that are inconsistent with the sensory reality and occur during semiconscious dominance.

Dreaming—subconscious process that updates the brain and mind with information that was collected during conscious dominance.

Dynamic thinking—flexible and unbiased way of thinking that considers all nemoniks equally and applies the ones that fit the actual situation.

Dyslexia—impairment in reading ability not resulting from low intelligence.

E

Educated—person who is in the possession of knowledge.

Education—mental process that transfers systematically detailed knowledge and skills from a teacher to a student.

Efficiency—achieving success with a minimum of effort and resources.

Einstein, Albert (1879-1955)—Swiss scientist who published in 1905 three papers that revolutionized Newtonian physics.

Emotive thinking—subconscious way of thinking that convinces the conscious with emotions that a particular description of reality is either true or false regardless of the presented evidence.

Entropy—decrease of order in a closed system. In simple words, things in the sensory reality will always decay. See Second Law of Thermodynamics.

EQ—Emotional Quotient, which provides insight in one's emotional intelligence.

ESP—extrasensory perception.

Exhaustive—complete, all-inclusive, and comprehensive in reference to the mind, sensory reality, and their interaction. Nemonik thinking is an exhaustive way of thinking that includes all options.

DIAGRAM OF THE EXTERNAL REALITY

<table>
<tr><td colspan="3">External Reality</td></tr>
<tr><td rowspan="2">Sensory</td><td colspan="2">Extrasensory</td></tr>
<tr><td>Scientific</td><td>Supernatural</td></tr>
<tr><td>known</td><td>unknown</td><td>unknowable</td></tr>
<tr><td colspan="3">Internal Reality</td></tr>
</table>

External reality—material and immaterial phenomena that surround the mind. The external reality comprises the sensory and extrasensory realities. The extrasensory reality comprises the scientific and supernatural realities. The subconscious creates the internal, constructed, or simulated reality from the external reality.

Extrasensory reality—part of the external reality that cannot be perceived through the natural human senses. The extrasensory reality comprises the scientific and supernatural realities.

F

Facts—testable descriptions of reality that are supported adequately by sensory perception and reason. Facts can be divided into natural and artificial facts.

False—description of reality that is inconsistent with the sensory reality.

Formal logic—part of reason that submits facts to validity rules in order to evaluate the truth of logical arguments and draw true conclusions, which become new facts.

Freud, Sigmund (1856-1939)—pioneer of Western psychology who introduced the psychoanalysis of the subconscious.

G

Genius—most able part of the mind that is hidden in the subconscious.

Goal—intended individual or collective achievement, which could be either a mission or a target.

Greed—accumulation for the sake of accumulation.

Groupthink—collective mental process rejecting correct information in order to protect incorrect information that is already accepted by the collective as true.

Guderian, Heinz Wilhelm (1888-1954)—German Panzer General who introduced the concept of Blitzkrieg.

Guilford, Joy Paul (1897-1987)—US psychologist who developed Guilford's cube and introduced the concepts of convergent and divergent thinking.

H

Habituation – mental process that derives mindsets from repetitive actions and thoughts.

Hallucination—non-sensory distortion of the internal reality associated with an imaginary external phenomenon.

Hard-drive—main memory device of a computer.

Hegel, Frederich (1770-1831)—German philosopher who introduced a dialectic describing the progress of knowledge. During the first stage, an opinion or thesis is challenged by a conflicting opinion or antithesis. This results in a mental conflict between the opponents. During the second stage, this conflict is resolved into an agreement between the opponents. This agreement is the synthesis between thesis and antithesis. The synthesis becomes the new thesis and the process repeats itself. Each new thesis provides an improvement over the previous one.

Humphrey, Albert S. (1926-2005)—American business consultant who introduced the SWOT-analysis.

Hypnosis—mental process during which a hypnotist evokes a deep relaxation in a participant and then makes suggestions that change the internal reality of that participant. After completing the changes, the hypnotist voices suggestion to restore conscious dominance. The suggestions to change remain effective after the subject is woken up by the hypnotist.

Hypothesis—testable description of reality that is not subjected to reason yet. Hypotheses include assumptions, postulations, presumptions, tenets, theories, etc. Facts and beliefs differ from hypotheses.

I

Illusion—incorrect sensory perception of a phenomenon in the sensory reality that is maintained by the subconscious in the face of contrasting reason.

Incubation period virus—time between the initial exposure to that virus and the first appearance of its symptoms. The incubation period of the CS7-virus equals the duration required for the educational indoctrination of conventional thinking.

Inductive thinking—conscious way of thinking that generalizes or extrapolates facts in order to reach a conclusion. It moves from multiple observations to a particular case. The resulting *'facts'* provide evidence, but no absolute proof for the conclusion.

Informal logic—part of reason that might be based on former formal logic that the reactive mindmode has transformed into mindsets.

Information management—ability to manage the perception and projection of information in order to maximize success.

Information overload—counterproductive awareness of processing consciously too much information.

Inner team—imaginary team of nemonik experts comprising the stereotypes of a scientist, judge, inventor, and computer programmer. They represent respectively the objective, collective, creative, and reactive mindmodes. Visualizing the stereotypes will foster an internal dialogue and, therefore, fosters thinking.

Inorganic—lifeless matter such as iron, rock, and water.

Instrument or Organon—book comprising ideas of Aristotle, which were compiled by the Peripatetics.

Interaction—effect of the mind on reality and vice versa. Whatever you do affects reality, while reality affects you. Reality is like a mirror that reflects your behaviour, which is called '*karma*'. The exhaustive components of interaction are *perception* and *projection.*

Interactive nemoniks—nemoniks that deal with the interaction between the mind and reality. The four interactive nemoniks are *accept, reject, reveal, and conceal.*

Internal reality—subjective spatial, material, and temporal conscious perception of the external reality that is created by the subconscious.

Intuition—reactive affecters that are created from information stored in the subconscious in order to protect the conscious from information overload.

Intuitive thinking—subconscious way of reactive thinking that convinces the conscious with reactive affecters that a particular description of reality is either true or false without providing the underlying reason.

IQ—Intelligence Quotient, which provides allegedly insight in one's intelligence.

Irrational—negative label to discredit non-rational or affectorial thinking.

J

Judge—stereotype of nemonik thinking representing the collective mindmode in the nemonik inner team.

Judgement-calls—decisions about risk-avoidance and risk-taking without sufficient conscious information.

K

Karma—repayment of your actions.

Koan—riddles used in Zen Buddhism, which have no rational solution.

L

Lao Zi (570-490 BC)—Chinese sage and philosopher who wrote about two-and-half thousand years ago the book *Dao De Jing*. Lao Zi was the first philosopher who made a distinction between objective and collective thinking. *Dao* (The Way of Nature) refers to objective thinking, while *De* (The Way of People) refers to collective thinking. Lao Zi advocated natural virtue and rejected the Confucian artificial virtue. Lao Zi's real name might have been Li Ehr, who was a historian in the state Chu. However, scholars disagree about the personal details of Lao Zi.

Lateral thinking—way of creative thinking that reformulates problems and looks at them from different perspectives in order to find solutions. Edward de Bono introduced this way of thinking in his book *'Lateral Thinking' (1970)*. The opposite of lateral thinking is vertical or rational thinking. Lateral thinking is part of the creative mindmode of nemonik thinking.

Lax decision criterion—criterion that will accept information easily. The advantage of a lax decision criterion is that you accept most of the true information.

Leaders—people who determine their own goals, take full authority and responsibility, create productive conditions, and convince others to support their goals.

Linear thinking—systematic, directive, and step-by-step way of thinking that inhibits diversions and follows a predetermined narrow path to solve a problem.

Listening—process of perceiving audio information.

Logical argument—part of formal logic that contains a set of facts leading to an irrefutable conclusion that becomes a new fact.

Logical thinking—part of rational thinking that uses critical thinking, deductive thinking, inductive thinking, formal logic, and informal logic in order to test the truth of descriptions of reality.

Lorenz, Edward (1917-2008)—American mathematician and meteorologist who, in 1963, introduced *Chaos Theory*, which holds that the universe is a deterministic chaos. Although the universe might be a deterministic system, small differences in the initial conditions cause unpredictable outcomes or chaos. Lorenz called this the butterfly effect.

M

Main mental bias—preference for either rational or affectorial thinking.

Managers—people who are responsible for their personal performance and that of their team.

Mantra—repeated voiced or unvoiced phrase, word, or sound that fosters semiconscious dominance by inhibiting unintentional conscious thoughts.

Material—refers to matter.

Matter—three-dimensional finite part of reality that features substance, volume, and weight, and occupies and moves through space and time. Matter is wrapped up energy that is determined by four features: density, volume, shape, and motion.

Meditation—intentional mental process that fosters concentration on relaxation. Meditation fosters semiconscious dominance by focusing consciously on a particular aspect of the internal reality, which inhibits unintentional conscious thoughts. A person in meditation maintains continuously a delicate balance between conscious and subconscious dominance. See Mind (Diagram), Concentration, Relaxation, Hypnosis, and Nemonik meditation.

Memory—self-organising and associative mental process that stores, maintains, and recalls information in order to preserve it across space and time.

Mental—refers to the mind.

Mental bias—cognitive distortion that is caused by a consistent preference for a specific way of thinking. As the Universe is dynamic, any mental bias will sooner or later become counterproductive.

Mental disorganization—used by the creative mindmode to generate creative affecters by unfreezing, disorganizing, reorganizing, and refreezing the memorized information.

Mental immune system—subconscious mental system that protects the information that is already accepted by the mind as correct. However, that protection becomes malignant when the mind protects incorrect information. The mental immune system uses cognitive dissonance and groupthink.

Mental nemoniks—nemoniks that refer to a particular mindmode. They are the *objective, collective, creative, and reactive mindmode.*

Mental processes—processes of the mind such as thinking, memory, contemplation, awareness, emotions, feelings, creativity, reason, intuition, sense perception, conception, judgment and understanding.

Mental reconstruction—subconscious reconstruction of the objective sensory reality into the conscious subjective internal reality.

Mental state—distinct level of awareness such as conscious dominance, subconscious dominance, semiconscious dominance, and unconsciousness.

Mental structures—relatively permanent parts of the mind such as the conscious, semiconscious, and subconscious.

Meta-thinking—thinking about the way we think. Hence, studying nemonik thinking is a way of meta-thinking.

DIAGRAM OF THE MIND

<table>
<tr><td colspan="5">Diagram of the Mind</td></tr>
<tr><td colspan="2">Conscious</td><td>Semiconscious</td><td colspan="2">Subconscious</td></tr>
<tr><td colspan="2">Concentration</td><td>Meditation</td><td colspan="2">relaxation</td></tr>
<tr><td colspan="2">Rational thinking</td><td rowspan="2"></td><td colspan="2">Affectorial thinking</td></tr>
<tr><td>Objective</td><td>Collective</td><td>Creative</td><td>Reactive</td></tr>
</table>

Mind—nonmaterial part of a person that comprises the total of all conscious, subconscious, and semiconscious mental structures and processes. The mind is abstract and can only exist in the extrasensory reality, because you cannot see, hear, taste, smell, or touch the mind. The mind is a theoretical construct that exists paradoxically in the mind. Nevertheless, this elusive construct helps us to evaluate our way of thinking. A healthy mind has a will, purpose, or intent that maintains goals such as maximizing success, obtaining comfort, escaping discomfort, and sustaining survival. Furthermore, it has abilities to think and memorize, and to maintain a productive interaction with the external reality. The mind has to deal with the order and chaos of reality. Therefore, the mind generates respectively rational thinking and affectorial thinking. See diagram.

Mind management—conscious management of the subconscious mind. Mind managements targets pain, emotions, motivation, attitude, emergency responses, intuitions, gut feelings etc.

Mind map—diagram showing the relationship between concepts that fosters understanding. Mind, body and spirit—holistic entity that cannot be split without losing some of its characteristics. The precise divisions between mind body and spirit are still unclear, because none of these entities can be studied in isolation.

Mindmode—specific way of thinking that deals with a specific aspect of the external reality. They comprise the *objective, collective, creative, and reactive mindmodes.* Each mindmode is an elementary way of thinking that has evolved as a result of natural environmental pressure. They are defined by different interactions between the order and chaos of the mental process versus the order and chaos of reality. (1) The objective mindmode uses mental order to deal with the natural order of reality. (2) The collective mindmode uses mental order to deal with the artificial order of reality. (3) The creative mindmode uses mental disorganization or chaos to deal with the chaos of reality. (4) The reactive mindmode uses mental order to deal with the chaos of reality.

Mindmode-analysis—evaluates the exhaustive interactions of the four mental nemoniks with the thirteen operational nemoniks in order to find the nemoniks that provide the *Best Fit* for the actual situation.

Mindsets—internalized sets of rules that are derived by the reactive mindmode from the past, the known, or experience in order to generate reactive affecters. Initially, mindsets are created by your conscious and stored in your subconscious. Every repetitive action or thought becomes ultimately a mindset. The reactive mindmode generates mindsets through the process of habituation. In computer science, mindsets could be compared to algorithms. The aim of mindsets is to increase our speed and accuracy of our decisions and actions by using pre-programmed instructions.

Mindware—hypothetical set of nonmaterial self-organizing processes that creates and maintains the mind. Mindware could be compared to the software of a computer. Mindware is learned and, therefore, the nurtured component of thinking. Mindware is supported by brainware.

Minkowski, Hermann (1864-1909)—Professor at the Zurich Federal Institute of Technology and Einstein's tutor. He proclaimed that Einstein never bothered about mathematics and called him a *'lazy dog'*. Minkowski introduced a geometrical version of the special theory of relativity.

Mission—long-term or ultimate goal of a person or collective. My mission is to help people to become the best thinkers they can be.

Mission effectiveness—ability of a person or collective to accomplish its mission. Mission effectiveness is doing the right things right at the right time.

Mission statement—comprises the rationale for the actions of a person or group. It sets the group or person apart from other groups or persons.

Mnemonic—Greek word meaning memory aid.

Model of the mind—diagram that shows the important components of the mind and their main interactions. The nemonik model of the mind includes the conscious, subconscious, and semiconscious. It features the conscious objective and collective mindmodes, and the subconscious creative and reactive mindmodes.

Motivation—mental drive to maximize success.

N

Natural—refers to that part of reality that is not manmade.

Natural facts—unchangeable facts about nature.

Natural knowledge—knowledge about the laws of nature or the laws of physics. Natural knowledge is objective, unchangeable, and eternal.

Natural laws—objective descriptions of the unchangeable cause-effect relationships of nature or the laws of physics.

Nemonik accelerator—cognitive method that increases the speed of your thinking by fostering agreement during disagreement, while fostering disagreement during agreement.

Nemonik meditation—special type of meditation that uses visualizations and unvoiced mantras in order to improve affecters during semiconscious dominance. Nemonik meditation synthesizes auto-balance, visualizations, mantras, progressive relaxation, breathing management, conditioning, and positive affirmations. See Meditation.

Nemonik template—basis for nemonik thinking, which comprises the seventeen nemoniks. The template is a checklist to evaluate the actual situation or problem.

Nemonik thinking—exhaustive and systematic way of thinking that maximizes the probability of success by subjecting seventeen nemoniks to both rational and affectorial thinking. The supernatural is outside the scope of nemonik thinking. See diagram.

Nemonik accelerator—cognitive method that increases the speed of your thinking by fostering agreement during disagreement, while fostering disagreement during agreement. This tool is based on Hegel's dialectic.

Nemoniks—seventeen memorized keywords describing the exhaustive aspects of the mind, reality, and the interaction of the mind and reality, which prompt the memory to recall associated information. The seventeen nemoniks are: *objective, collective, creative, reactive, advance, stay, retreat, accumulate, preserve, dispose, act, wait, prepare, accept, reject, reveal, and conceal.* See diagram.

DIAGRAM OF NEMONIK THINKING

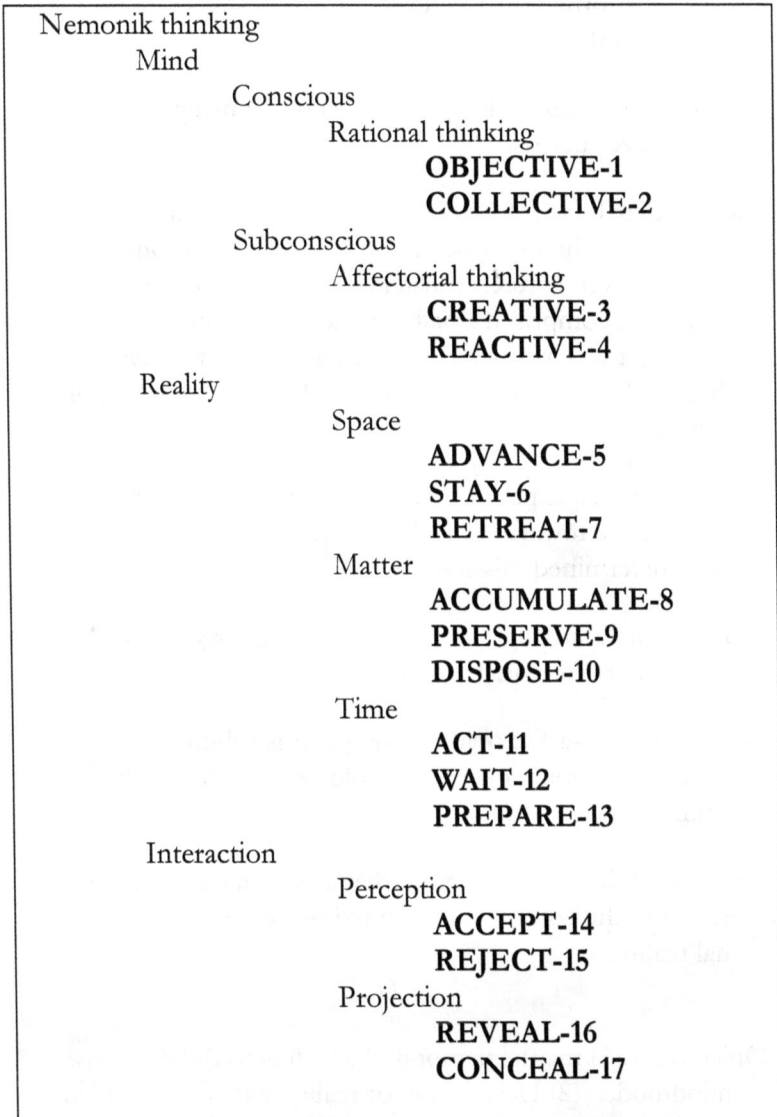

- Nemonik thinking
  - Mind
    - Conscious
      - Rational thinking
        - **OBJECTIVE-1**
        - **COLLECTIVE-2**
    - Subconscious
      - Affectorial thinking
        - **CREATIVE-3**
        - **REACTIVE-4**
  - Reality
    - Space
      - **ADVANCE-5**
      - **STAY-6**
      - **RETREAT-7**
    - Matter
      - **ACCUMULATE-8**
      - **PRESERVE-9**
      - **DISPOSE-10**
    - Time
      - **ACT-11**
      - **WAIT-12**
      - **PREPARE-13**
  - Interaction
    - Perception
      - **ACCEPT-14**
      - **REJECT-15**
    - Projection
      - **REVEAL-16**
      - **CONCEAL-17**

Nerve signals—uniform electrical-chemical signals carrying coded information about the sensory reality from the senses to the brain.

Networking—skill to foster personal relationships in order to maximize success.

Newton, Sir Isaac (1642-1727)—British mathematician and physicists who described in his book *Principia* some of the basic laws of nature. Einstein synthesized Newton's thesis that light comprised small particles with Young's antithesis that light was a wave. See First Law of Thermodynamics, Second Law of Thermodynamics, Third Law of Motion, and Scientists.

Non-directional expansion or organic expansion—growth of a collective towards available opportunities without having a predetermined mission.

Non-rational thinking—negative label to discredit non-rational or affectorial thinking.

Non-thinking—affectorial thinking that is subconscious thinking without conscious thinking. Antonym—Rational thinking.

Normal—collective judgement that a person's internal reality is within the collectively accepted perception of the external reality.

O

Objective—(1) mental nemonik that refers to the objective mindmode. (2) Description of reality that is independent of what anyone believes.

Objective mindmode—way of rational thinking that deals with the natural order of the sensory reality, which can be described by natural laws and facts that make nature predictable.

Objective specialists—found where proficiency in natural laws is crucial such as in science and technology.

Operating system—basic software that tells a set of electronic components how to act as a computer. Similarly, nemonik thinking is the operating system for the brain. It tells the brain how to act as a thinker.

Operational bias—mental distortion that is caused by a consistent preference for a specific operational nemonik.

Operational nemoniks—thirteen nemoniks comprising the nine reality nemoniks and the four interactive nemoniks.

Opportunity—potential advantage. For example, receiving a job offer is an opportunity. An opportunity is optional and the outcome depends on the decision of the person.

Order—part of the external reality that can be subjected to reason. It is associated with comprehensibility, knowledge, predictability, recognisability, etc. The mind developed conscious rational thinking to deal with the order of reality. Antonym—Chaos.

Organic—refers to matter that is alive such as animals, microbes, plants, and people.

Organizing—process of transforming chaos into order. Organizing is the allocation, integration, and movement of mental, spatial, material, temporal, and interactive resources into a unified system that is ready to carry out a plan. Organizing requires skills such as negotiation, promoting, and networking.

P

Panic—counterproductive conflict between the conscious and subconscious for mental dominance that paralysis the mind.

Peers—people who have a similar socio-economic background in common.

Perception—part of the nemonik interaction that manages the incoming information flow from the sensory reality towards the mind. The senses facilitate sensory perception by detecting incoming information. The exhaustive options provided by perception for maximizing success are to *Accept and Reject* information. Listening is an easy way to gain information.

Perfection—ability to maximize one's efficiency, speed, and accuracy in order to adjust to the changes in reality. As the sensory reality changes continuously, perfection is a process, rather than a state. Perfection is driven by the urge to survive.

Perseverance—persistent continuation of a course of action despite difficulties and obstacles.

Peter's principle—people will be promoted to their level of incompetence. A person who is doing a great job is most likely to be promoted. Promotions stop when that person fails in the higher job. Hence, ultimately, all employees will occupy jobs they cannot handle. That is counterproductive for both the individual and the team.

Philosopher—means literally a lover of wisdom.

Philosophy—the pursuit of wisdom that is obtained by means of reasoning rather than by experimentation or faith. Philosophy is about general causes, principles and the human perception of reality.

Plan—mental or physical map describing the intended actions across time required to reach a predetermined goal. Plans include strategies and tactics.

Planning—comprehensive examination of the spatial, material, temporal, perceptive, and projective aspects of the situation with the four mindmodes in order to create a plan.

Positioning—ability to manoeuvre into a situation where the strategic advantage is so large that the opposition has to avoid a conflict at all cost. Sun Zi warns against rash actions: *'Competent generals do not fight'*. Any conflict will destroy resources on both sides.

Positive affirmation—phrase or sentence that improves the subconscious e.g.—*Each day I feel better.*

Prepare—temporal nemonik that prompts the mind to get ready for action.

Present—infinitesimal moment between the past and future that moves into the future with the speed of time.

Preserve—material nemonik that prompts the mind to maintain the same amount of matter that is under control.

Priority—task that is so urgent or important that it has to be completed before any other task.

Proactivity—productive early action that fosters opportunities and inhibits threats.

Problem solving—nemonik thinking is a problem solving tool. It uses the nemonik checklist to raise questions, create ideas, identifying problems, strengths, weaknesses, opportunities, and threats.

Procrastination—counterproductive delay of action that inhibits opportunities and fosters threats.

Programmer—stereotype of nemonik thinking representing the reactive mindmode in the nemonik inner team.

Progress—process that decreases the distance to the goal or alternatively, increases the distance from the edge of survival. In our era, progress is defined often as the advance of science and the application of increasingly advanced technologies.

Progressive relaxation—systematic and step-by-step process of alternating tension and relaxation of muscles. Progressive relaxation was introduced by Edmund Jacobson (1888-1983).

Projection—part of interaction that refers to managing the outgoing information flow from the mind towards the sensory reality. The exhaustive options provided by projection for maximizing success are to *Reveal and Conceal* information.

Prompting—using a memorized phrase or word (prompt) to recall associated information from the memory.

Q

R

RAM—Randomly Accessible Memory of a computer.

Rashness—fast but counterproductive decisions without adequate conscious thoughts or subconscious mindsets.

Rational bias—consistent preference for rational thinking that is independent of the sensory reality.

Rational deadlock—prolonged dispute in which the opponents fail to reach an agreement, because they are unable to synthesize the thesis and antithesis.

Rational thinking—conscious part of nemonik thinking that deals with the predictable order of reality by submitting facts to reason in order to create new facts. Rational thinking uses the mental order of reason to deal with the order of the sensory reality.

Rationalizing—corrupted version of rational thinking that provides pseudo -rational justifications to defend a previously made conclusion.

Rational-operations—part of rational thinking that comprises mental processes such as analysing, integrating, reorganizing, and interpreting.

Reactive—(1) mental nemonik referring to the reactive mindmode. (2) Mental or physical response without conscious thinking that is initiated by the reactive mindmode.

Reactive affecters—affecters that are generated by mindsets and deal with the chaos of reality.

Reactive mindmode—way of affectorial thinking that deals with the chaos of reality by habituating mindsets that generate reactive affecters.

Reactive specialists—found where individual perfection is crucial such as in chess, driving, martial arts, sports, surgery, etc.

Reality nemoniks—nemoniks that deal with the aspects of the sensory reality. The nine reality nemoniks are—*advance, stay, retreat, accumulate, preserve, dispose, act, wait, and prepare.*

Reality-check—critical evaluation with rational thinking whether a particular affecter fits the sensory reality.

Reality—See Sensory reality.

Reason—part of rational thinking that comprises formal logic and informal logic.

Recreation—conscious replacement of activities that are essential for success with nonessential activities.

Reductionism—reducing the number of variables in order to reduce the chaos of the external reality. The danger is that reductionists lose contact with the sensory reality of everyday life.

Reject—perceptual nemonik that prompts the mind to refuse the incoming information as a true description of the sensory reality.

Relaxation—mental process that fosters subconscious dominance by inhibiting involuntary conscious thoughts. Opposite—Concentration. See Meditation, Nemonik meditation, and Progressive relaxation.

Reliability—refers to the accuracy of measurement.

Reliable arguments—comprise only facts. In the argument (A > B, B > C, therefore A > C), (A should be indeed larger than B, while B should be indeed larger than C).

Religion—institution that promotes the belief in a divine power, which is regarded to be the creator and leader of the universe. Most religions aim to describe the unknowable.

REM sleep—stage of sleep characterized by Rapid-Eye-Movements and dreaming, which occupies about twenty per cent of the sleeping time.

Retreat—spatial nemonik that prompts the mind to increase the distance to the goal.

Reveal—projectional nemonik that prompts the mind to project true information to the sensory reality.

Righteous thinking—corrupted version of collective thinking that creates rights without obligations for privileged individuals within a collective.

Risk-management—process of evaluating, comparing, and controlling the potential advantages and disadvantages of an action in order to maximize the probability of success.

S

SCARRED—nemonik acronym that represents the seven main weaknesses of conventional thinking. **S**tatic, rather than dynamic thinking; **C**riticizing, rather than critical thinking; **A**nswering, rather than questioning; **R**ationalizing, rather than rational thinking; **R**ighteous, rather than collective; **E**ducated, rather than wise; **De**tached, rather than compassionate.

Science—body of valid and reliable descriptions concerning the external reality.

Scientific method—process based on analysis, experimentation, data collection, formal logic, generalization, mathematics, measurements, natural laws, literature reviews, samples, sensory observations, peer review, theorizing, reason, reliability tests, replicated results, statistical analyses, hypotheses tests, validity tests, etc.

Scientific reality—part of the extrasensory reality that can be perceived with artificial sensors or rational thinking.

Scientific reduction—reduction from the extrasensory reality to the scientific reality that is caused by the limitation of current knowledge.

Scientist—stereotype of a nemonik thinker representing the objective mindmode in the nemonik inner team. Famous scientists were Leonardo da Vinci, Nicolaus Copernicus, Sir Isaac Newton, Thomas Young, Hermann Minkowski, Albert Einstein, and Max Planck.

Scorched earth—military strategy to destroy everything during a retreat, so that the opponent cannot use those resources.

Second Law of Thermodynamics—entropy or chaos will always increase in a closed system, or alternatively, the order of a closed system will always decrease. In simple words, things will always decay. Order will be always transformed into chaos. This is an important law because it predicts that the future of our entire Universe will be ultimately a state of chaos. In contrast, Lao Zi's philosophy implies that the Universe is moving towards harmony. However, the difference might be in the definition of chaos.

Self—observer of a person's internal reality, which that person consciously calls 'I'. The Self of a healthy person is projected to the sensory reality through a set of relatively stable behavioural and mental characteristics.

Semiconscious—part of the mind that comprises parts of the conscious and subconscious, which form a communication channel between those parts of the mind.

Semiconscious dominance—healthy mental state that is fostered by meditation. This state fosters conscious awareness of subconscious activity. This state fosters the conscious improvement of the subconscious way of affectorial thinking.

Sensations—subconsciously created phenomena in the internal reality that are derived from phenomena in the sensory reality.

Senses—integrated physiological and mental systems that perceive material signals from the sensory reality and transform them into neural signals. The five traditional senses are hearing, seeing, smelling, tasting, and touching. However, people have also senses for balance, body position, movement, pain, pressure, temperature, etc.

Sensors—cells in the body that are able to detect sensory signals from the sensory reality and convert them into nerve signals.

Sensory perception—perception by the senses of material signals that are emitted by the sensory reality.

Sensory reality—part of the external reality that can be perceived directly through the natural human senses. If not otherwise indicated, *reality* means *sensory reality*.

Sensory reduction—reduction from the external reality to the sensory reality, which is caused by the natural limitations of the human senses.

Sensory signals—emitted or reflected by material objects within the sensory reality that can be detected by the senses. Sensory signals include pressure, heat, vibration, light, particles, etc.

Silent mind—mental state that is devoid of conscious thoughts and fosters subconscious action without conscious interference.

Sliding—mental process of shifting consciously the dominance window across the mental continuum.

Social control—controlling what citizens do and what they think. Social control maintains the fabric of our collective. Socialisation or indoctrination is the process by which the collective indoctrinates its members with the formal and informal rules of that collective.

Socrates (470-399 BC)—Greek philosopher, sculptor, and soldier from Athens who was the teacher of Plato and Xenophon.

Solution-oriented thinking—focusses on producing correct solutions without sufficiently evaluating the significance of the problems. Solution-oriented thinking might find the right answer for the wrong question.

Space—three-dimensional, infinite, and nonmaterial part of reality in which matter is immersed and moves around. Space provides the exhaustive options to *Advance, Stay, and Retreat.*

Spatial—refers to space.

Spatial dimensions—latitude, longitude, and altitude. Together, those coordinates can determine any unique position in space.

Specialists—peak performers in their field of operation who are exclusively responsible for their personal performance.

Spencer, Herbert (1820-1903)—English philosopher who introduced the important distinctions between the *known, unknown, and unknowable.*

Spirit—hypothetical nonmaterial part of a person that allegedly provides life to the material body. The spirit is part of the supernatural reality and is therefore excluded from nemonik thinking.

Static thinking—rigid and biased way of thinking that considers only preselected nemoniks and applies those independent of the actual situation.

Stay—spatial nemonik that prompts the mind to maintain the same distance to the goal.

Strategical thinking—way of thinking that produces strategies. Strategical thinking is incorporated in nemonik thinking.

Strategy—plan to complete a mission, while tactics are detailed plans of that strategy.

Strength—intrinsic advantage.

Strict decision criterion—criterion that will reject information easily.

Subconscious—large part of the mind that is continuously active outside the conscious awareness of that person. The subconscious is associated with sleep, relaxation, knowledge, genius, internal reality, and affectorial thinking. The prime aim of the subconscious is to protect the conscious from an information overload.

Subconscious dominance—healthy mental state that is fostered by relaxation. During this state, the subconscious is active, while the conscious is inhibited. The aim of this state is mental and physical recuperation.

Subjective descriptions—description of reality that depends on the beliefs and perceptions of the particular individual.

Success—*obtain what you seek and escape what you suffer (Lao Zi).* Some people might seek fame, freedom, knowledge, power, safety, skills, wealth, etc. The aim of nemonik thinking is maximizing the probability of success. Therefore, nemonik thinking is goal oriented and fosters compassion, allies, and win-win strategies.

Successive approximation—cyclic process that moves each turn closer towards the ultimate goal.

Sun Zi (554-496 BC)—Chinese warrior-philosopher who wrote about two-and-half thousand years ago the book—*Bingfa or The Art of War.*

Supernatural reality—part of the extrasensory reality that is outside the scientific reality. The supernatural reality includes such phenomena as clairvoyance, divine power, ESP, extrasensory perception, God, paranormal, precognition, PSI, psychokinesis, spirit, telekinesis, and telepathy.

Survival—process of staying alive, which is the first step of success.

SWOT-analysis—problem solving tool that evaluates the *Strengths, Weaknesses, Opportunities, and Threats* of each nemonik in comparison to the actual situation. *Strength* is an intrinsic advantage; *Weakness* is an intrinsic disadvantage; *Opportunity* is a potential advantage; and *Threat* is a potential disadvantage. For example, having a university degree is a strength, but receiving a job offer is an opportunity. Having thin bones is a weakness, but the possibility of breaking a leg during skiing is a threat. The SWOT-analysis was introduced by the American business consultant Albert S. Humphrey (1926-2005).

Synergy—additional output that is generated when the interaction between the parts is more than their simple sum.

Synthesis—description of reality that merges a thesis and an antithesis into a new thesis. A synthesis might create synergy.

System dependency—over-reliance on organizations, hierarchies, and bureaucracies.

Systems thinking—part of conventional thinking that considers reality to comprise dynamic systems, which influence each other in order to maximize their success. A collective is such a system.

T

Tactic—plan to complete a target in order to maximize success.

Tactical thinking—way of thinking that produces tactics in order to maximize success.

Target—short-term goal that could be a step towards the completion of a mission.

Technocrats—people who apply scientific knowledge to develop artefacts such as tools, machines, and computers that increase our control over the environment.

Technology—knowledge and application of artificial manipulation of organic and inorganic matter into artefacts. In our collective, people often regard progress to be the advance of science and the application of more advanced technologies.

Temporal—refers to time.

The Art of War or Bing Fa—book about strategy written by Sun Zi about two-and-half thousand years ago. Although written about war, Sun Zi's advice applies also to daily life.

Thesis—tested description of reality.

Thinking—self-organizing mental process that recalls, evaluates, transforms, and generates information.

Threat—potential disadvantage. A threat is optional and the outcome depends on the decision of the person.

Time—one-dimensional, eternal, and nonmaterial part of reality that can be perceived indirectly by changes in matter and the movement of matter through space. Time provides the exhaustive nemoniks to *Act, Wait, and Prepare.*

Timing—execution of an action at the most productive moment.

Transformation—simultaneous accumulation of one type of matter by disposing another type of matter.

True—description of reality that is consistent with the sensory reality.

True arguments—consistent, reliable, and valid logical arguments.

U

Unconsciousness—unhealthy mental state that is characterized by a persistent unawareness of the sensory reality and the Self. Unconsciousness differs from subconscious dominance, because you will not wake up in case of danger. Hence, unconsciousness could be seen as a suspension of life. Unconsciousness could be caused by physical or mental traumas, analgesics, asphyxiation, and toxic substances.

Universal Law of Causality—natural law that prevails in daily life and holds that the same natural cause always precedes the same natural effect. This law assumes order in the Universe.

Unrealistic thinking—way of thinking that is inconsistent with the sensory reality. Unrealistic thinking differs from non-rational thinking.

V

Valid arguments—comprise facts that are related to the conclusion that they intend to support. In the argument (A > B, B > C, therefore ...), (A > X would be an invalid conclusion, because X is not mentioned in the facts).

Validity—measure of how well a theory applies to the topic of that theory. Validity refers to measuring the correct variable.

Vertical thinking—way of rational thinking that solves problems by overcoming obstacles in the chosen line of approach. This concept was introduced by Edward de Bono as the opposite of lateral thinking.

Virus—small entity that lives in a host and is concealed, self-replicating, and self-protective. A benign virus lives in symbiosis within its host, while a malignant virus destroys its host.

Visualization—mental picture that is consciously maintained in the internal reality in order to inhibit unintentional conscious thoughts during mediation.

W

Wait—temporal nemonik that prompts the mind to delay an action until it is the right time for that action.

Weakness—intrinsic disadvantage. For example, having thin bones is a weakness.

Winning—defeating opponents in competition and, therefore, winning is conflict oriented, which fosters control, force, aggression, enemies, and win-lose strategies. The aim of conventional thinking is maximizing the probability of winning.

Wisdom—productive application of knowledge to the actual situation. Wisdom is our mental resonance with nature.

X

Y

Young, Thomas (1773-1829)—conducted the famous double-split experiment that supported the widely accepted antithesis that light moves through space like a wave. This antithesis contradicted Newton's thesis that light comprised small particles. Einstein synthesized those ideas.

Z

Zen Buddhism—school of Buddhism that developed in China and spread later to Japan. The aim of Zen is to see the world as it is. Live in the now and here. The ultimate state of nirvana can be reached in a single lifetime, rather than in a succession of value accumulating lives.

EXERCISE WWI (PART 1)

The aim of this exercise is to compare your way of thinking before and after you study this manual. This will provide you with information about your cognitive improvement.

It is in your interest to stretch your mind by thinking about extreme situations. If you can handle those extremes, then you can transform daily weaknesses into strengths and threats into opportunities. One of the most extreme situations is war. War is abhorrent and one of the greatest threats to your survival and that of our species. Nevertheless, it deserves attention because it shows clearly the extremes of human thinking. War is like a looking glass that magnifies the mental strategies we use in daily life. War cannot be stopped by ignoring it. In contrast, if you study war, then you might be able to avoid it. In accord, the Chinese warrior-philosopher Sun Zi (~6th c. BC) wrote about two-and-half thousand years ago in his book *Bing Fa* or *The Art of War—Competent generals do not fight.*[154]

For the sake of this exercise, imagine that you are a highly decorated four-star general who has just arrived in the trenches on a battlefield during the First World War. By the way, congratulations with your instant promotion. Unfortunately, you do not know the situation yet, but your subordinate officers advise you unanimously—*Act right now and order the advance!*

I invite you to spend ten minutes on writing an evaluation of their advice. Keep it short and simple. You are in the middle of a battle! The opportunity to advance might slip away and could turn into a threat! Time is crucial. Your officers are waiting for your decision. This might be a difficult exercise, but if it were easy, then this manual would not be worth reading. Later, we will come back to your written evaluation. Success with your new job!

Notes

EXERCISES NEMONIK MEDITATION

PREPARATION

WARNING

Nemonik meditation is a powerful mental tool. Therefore, handle it with wisdom and care. Do not use nemonik meditation when you need to be awake and alert. For example, do not use it when driving a car or when using machinery. You might become drowsy and cause an accident.

Worrying fosters conscious dominance, which is counterproductive for nemonik meditation, because it inhibits semiconscious dominance. Therefore, make in advance a to-do-list of anything that you have to attend to after the session. In that way, you do not have to worry during the session about something you might forget. Semiconscious dominance fosters your creative mindmode and, therefore, you might get ideas during the session. To inhibit unintentional conscious thoughts, it might be better to interrupt your session temporarily and write those ideas down. Otherwise, you might keep thinking about them. So, keep pen and paper at hand.

It is easier to start your first session in a quiet location with dimmed lights. Switch off your phone etc. Ask others not to interrupt you or put a note on the door to that effect. Some people prefer soft continuous background sound such as classical music or an off-station radio in order to mask intrusive noises. Later you will learn to foster semiconscious dominance without such external aids.

Make yourself comfortable and lie down on a bed or sit down in an easy chair. Do not try to freeze your body during any stage of your meditation. Just keep moving around until you feel comfortable. Otherwise, your focus will be distracted by discomfort. Meditative immobility might decrease your body temperature. Therefore, make sure that you stay warm.

If you have only limited time for your session, then it might be a good idea to set an alarm.

Nemonik meditation is a mental process that reaches semi-conscious dominance by avoiding both conscious and sub-conscious dominance. That process is intentional and, therefore, it has to be directed by the conscious. Hence, you should try to stay awake during your meditation session. When you fall asleep, you reach subconscious dominance and the meditation stops automatically. Do not worry! If you have fallen asleep, then you will wake up in the normal way. You might have needed the sleep more than the meditation. Just try again. If you lose track during any meditation session, just restart where you lost track. Do not be too hard on yourself—Take it easy—Go with the flow—Meditation should be fun!

You can meditate as many times as you want and as long as you like, but do not force it. During your training period, meditate at least one session a day. Be patient—do not rush through the exercises. Repeat each exercise daily until you can complete it automatically and without falling asleep. At least repeat the exercise for one week. It might be helpful to complete a few sessions of each exercise with open eyes, so that you can learn the instructions.

PREPARATION

Make to-do list.
Find suitable location.
Prevent interruptions.
Be comfortable.
Stay awake.
Set alarm.

LEGEND

These symbols prevent repetitions of text in the instructions for the exercises.

<table>
<tr><td>(...)</td><td>General instructions.</td></tr>
<tr><td><...></td><td>Inhale unforced.</td></tr>
<tr><td>>...<</td><td>Exhale unforced.</td></tr>
<tr><td><<...>></td><td>Inhale deeply expanding your tummy.</td></tr>
<tr><td>>>...<<</td><td>Exhale slowly and let it all go.</td></tr>
<tr><td>>mantra<</td><td>Unvoiced or silent mantra.</td></tr>
<tr><td>|</td><td>Change from inhaling to exhaling.</td></tr>
<tr><td>| |</td><td>Hold your breath for a moment.</td></tr>
<tr><td>(5x)</td><td>Repeat about 5 times.</td></tr>
<tr><td>(5 min)</td><td>Repeat about 5 minutes.</td></tr>
</table>

EXERCISE 1: BASICS

The aim of this basic exercise is to acquire the skills to start and finish a nemonik meditation session adequately. The start fosters semiconscious dominance, while the finish fosters conscious dominance and inhibits post meditative drowsiness. The instructions to clench, unclench, stretch, and relax your extremities, foster your awareness of hidden muscle tension. The exercise synchronizes your breathing pattern with the silent mantras, while fostering relaxation. The mantra *-I am calm and relaxed-* is repeated for about five minutes in order to condition that mantra with the obtained mental state of semiconscious dominance. At a later stage, this mantra will be used to shorten the exercise significantly.

FEATURES

Muscle relaxation
Unvoiced mantras
Self-suggestions
Breathing management

EXERCISE 1: BASICS[xii]

(START)

(Close your eyes)

(Clench and unclench slowly your fists (5x))

(Stretch and relax slowly your arms and legs (5x))

<<...>> || >>...<< (3x)

<<At three>> | >>I am relaxed<<

<one> | >relax<

<two> | >relax<

<three> | >relax<

<I am> | >calm and relaxed< (5 min)

(FINISH)

<<At one>> | >>I am wide awake<<

<<three>> | >>awake<<

<<two>> | >>awake<<

<<one>> | >>awake<<

<<I am>> | >>wide awake <<

(Open your eyes)

If you feel still drowsy after the session, then repeat vigorously the FINISH of the exercise with eyes open.

[xii] See the previous legend for the symbols.

EXERCISE 2: THUMB

Make sure that you master the previous exercise first. The aim of this exercise is to relax the thumb of your dominant hand. The thumb is a small part of your body and relaxing it is an achievable goal even when you are tense. A relaxed body is incompatible with a tense mind. Therefore, relaxing the thumb will force the mind to relax. If necessary, select another small part of your body.

Use the start and finish of exercise 1. The mantra—*My thumb is relaxed*—is part of the progressive relaxation. Focus your entire mind on your thumb. If you are distracted, do not worry. Just bring your mind back to the exercise. Similar to exercise 1, the mantra -*I am calm and relaxed*- is repeated for about five minutes in order to condition that mantra with the obtained mental state of semiconscious dominance.

FEATURES

Muscle relaxation
Unvoiced mantras
Self-suggestions
Breathing management
Progressive relaxation (thumb)

EXERCISE 2: THUMB

(START)

<My thumb> | >is relaxed< (3x)

<I am> | >calm and relaxed< (5 min)

(FINISH)

EXERCISE 3: UPPER BODY

Make sure that you master the previous exercise first. The aim of this exercise is to spread the progressive relaxation from your thumb to the upper part of your body. Move slowly from one body part to the next. A relaxed body is incompatible with a tense mind. Therefore, relaxing the body will force the mind to relax. Focus your entire mind on the body part that you are relaxing.

FEATURES

Muscle relaxation
Unvoiced mantras
Self-suggestions
Breathing management
Progressive relaxation (thumb)
Progressive relaxation (upper body)

EXERCISE 3: UPPER BODY

(START)

<My thumb> | >is relaxed< (3x)
<My hands> | >are relaxed< (3x)
<My arms> | >are relaxed< (3x)
<My shoulders> | >are relaxed< (3x)
<My neck> | >is relaxed< (3x)
<My chest> | >is relaxed< (3x)

<I am> | >calm and relaxed< (5 min)

(FINISH)

EXERCISE 4: LOWER BODY

Make sure that you master the previous exercise first. The aim of this exercise is to spread the progressive relaxation through the lower part of your body. A relaxed body is incompatible with a tense mind. Therefore, relaxing the body will force the mind to relax.

FEATURES

Muscle relaxation
Unvoiced mantras
Self-suggestions
Breathing management
Progressive relaxation (thumb)
Progressive relaxation (upper body)
Progressive relaxation (lower body)

EXERCISE 4: LOWER BODY

(START)

<My thumb> | >is relaxed< (3x)
<My hands> | >are relaxed< (3x)
<My arms> | >are relaxed< (3x)
<My shoulders> | >are relaxed< (3x)
<My neck> | >is relaxed< (3x)
<My chest> | >is relaxed< (3x)
<My abdomen> | >is relaxed< (3x)
<My legs> | >are relaxed< (3x)
<My feet> | >are relaxed< (3x)

<I am> | >calm and relaxed< (5 min)

(FINISH)

EXERCISE 5: FACE

Make sure that you master the previous exercise first. The aim of this exercise is facial relaxation. Your face is an important tool to communicate your state of mind to other people. A relaxed face is incompatible with a tense mind. Therefore, relaxing the face will force the mind to relax.

FEATURES

Muscle relaxation
Unvoiced mantras
Self-suggestions
Breathing management
Progressive relaxation (entire body)
Progressive relaxation (face)

EXERCISE 5: FACE

(START)

<My entire body> | >is relaxed< (3x)
<My lips> | >are relaxed< (3x)
<My eyes> | >are relaxed< (3x)
<My forehead> | >is relaxed< (3x)
<My jaw> | >is relaxed< (3x)
<My entire face> | >is relaxed< (3x)

<I am> | >calm and relaxed< (5 min)

(FINISH)

EXERCISE 6: ENTIRE BODY

Make sure that you master the previous exercise first. The aim of this exercise is to spread the progressive relaxation through your entire body. During the mantra -*My entire body is relaxed*- imagine that the relaxation of your thumb spread throughout your entire body part by part. A relaxed body is incompatible with a tense mind. Therefore, relaxing the body will force the mind to relax.

FEATURES

Muscle relaxation
Unvoiced mantras
Self-suggestions
Breathing management
Progressive relaxation (thumb)
Progressive relaxation (entire body)

EXERCISE 6: ENTIRE BODY

(START)

<My thumb> | >is relaxed< (3x)
<My entire body> | >is relaxed< (5 min)

<I am> | >calm and relaxed< (5 min)

(FINISH)

EXERCISE 7: DEEPENING

The aim of this exercise is to deepen the state of semiconscious dominance as far as possible without falling asleep. Just before falling asleep, many people become aware of a feeling of warmth and heaviness. In accord, this deepening exercise features the mantra-*I feel warm and heavy*-. Simultaneously, imagine a feeling of warmth and heaviness spreading through your body.

FEATURES

Muscle relaxation
Unvoiced mantras
Self-suggestions
Breathing management
Progressive relaxation (entire body)
Deepening

EXERCISE 7: DEEPENING

(START)

<My entire body> | >is relaxed< (3x)
<I feel> | >warm and heavy< (5 min)

<I am> | >calm and relaxed< (5 min)

(FINISH)

EXERCISE 8: POSITIVE AFFIRMATIONS

As mentioned, positive affirmations are mantras that improve affecters in order to maximize the probability of success. I do not know your circumstances and, therefore, you might have to create your own mantras. The lyrics of songs might provide inspiration. Be careful not to use negative words in your mantras, because they reinforce negativity in your subconscious. Use only one mantra at the time. The following mantras might give you some inspiration:

<I am> | >a champion<
<I am> | >confident<
<I am> | >successful<
<I am> | >healthy and happy<
<I am> | >cool, calm and collected<
<I feel> | >stronger and stronger<
<I feel> | >better and better<
<I will> | >survive<

FEATURES

Muscle relaxation
Unvoiced mantras
Self-suggestions
Breathing management
Progressive relaxation (entire body)
Deepening
Positive affirmations

EXERCISE 8: POSITIVE AFFIRMATIONS

(START)
<<At three>> | >>I am relaxed<<
<one> | >relax<
<two> | >relax<
<three> | >relax<
<I am> | >calm and relaxed< (5x)

(Positive affirmation) (5 min)

(FINISH)
<<At one>> | >>I am wide awake<<
<<three>> | >>awake<<
<<two>> | >>awake<<
<<one>> | >>awake<<
<<I am>> | >>wide awake <<
(Open your eyes)

HYPNOSIS

Hypnosis is a mental process during which a hypnotist evokes a deep relaxation in a participant and then makes suggestions that change the internal reality of that participant. A cloud of secrecy and mystery surrounds the ancient art of hypnotism. However, hypnosis is a natural process that is only mysterious if you want it to be mysterious. The hypnotist has no mysterious powers over the participant. Instead, the hypnotist uses the mindpower of the participant to guide that person into a deep relaxation. Hypnosis happens entirely in the mind of the participant.

Everyone is hypnotized many times in his or her life. For example, if a child has a tummy ache, the mother will try to relax the child. She might suggest that everything is all right and that the doctor will come in a few minutes. However, if she is not a doctor herself, then she does not know whether things are all right. The child might have eaten something poisonous. The mother might not even know if the doctor will come. Nevertheless, the child has unlimited trust in the mother and will internalize her suggestions. The child feels better, because the mother has changed the internal reality of the child with her positive suggestions. The child is hypnotized in a natural way by the mother. There is nothing mysterious about it!

Hypnosis can have the same positive effects as meditation. However, hypnosis can be sometimes more effective, because meditation has its limits. During meditation, the participant has to maintain semiconscious dominance in order to deliver consciously the suggestions that improve his or her internal reality. If the semiconscious dominance is shifted too far to the subconscious, it will become impossible for the conscious to make those all-important suggestions. Meditation is limited by the trade-off between the depth of relaxation and the conscious ability to make suggestions. Therefore, meditation might not be strong enough to make the required improvements. In contrast, a hypnotist could guide the participant towards a deeper state of relaxation, while the hypnotist remains able to make the required suggestions. Hence, hypnosis could be seen as assisted meditation.

Hypnosis is a matter of the greatest trust. It could be dangerous, because the participant let the hypnotist pass his or her conscious, which is the critic of the mind. After obtaining entry to the subconscious, the hypnotist has considerable power to change the internal reality of the participant. Hence, the participant has to trust his or her most precious possession to the hypnotist. Sometimes, you might need a hypnotherapist to improve something deep in your mind. However, be very careful whom you invite to enter your mind. Be aware of people who claim to have special powers. They might try to take away yours.

DREAMING

Dreams have fascinated people for thousands of years. Sleep research supports the notion that everyone dreams during periods of Rapid-Eye-Movements (REM) sleep. REM sleep occupies about twenty per cent of the sleeping time. People who are woken up during such sleep are likely to remember their dreams, even if they do not remember them usually. This suggests that everyone dreams and that it fulfils a basic mental need. Nevertheless, some people remember their dreams vividly, while others report that they never dream. Consequently, there is a difference between dreaming and dream awareness.

When you are awake and active, your mind needs to work optimally in order to maximize your success. At the same time, a continuous stream of new information enters your mind. However, you cannot stop your activities in order to update your mind with that information, because that would immobilize your mind in the middle of action. Therefore, it makes sense to assume that the incoming information is temporarily stored in a kind of buffer memory. During your sleep, that memory would be emptied and the new information would be integrated in the complex structure of your mind. Therefore, I propose that dreaming is a subconscious process that updates the brain and mind with information that was collected during conscious dominance. In that sense, dreaming is a pragmatic process that fosters your success.

Any awareness of a subconscious process requires conscious involvement. Dreams that occur during subconscious dominance are by definition inaccessible to your conscious. Hence, dream awareness can only occur during semiconscious dominance. Dream awareness is the conscious awareness of subconscious dreams that are inconsistent with the sensory reality and occur during semiconscious dominance.

Dreaming might synthesize important information, which could induce the subconscious to alert the conscious by sliding to semiconscious dominance. In that way, you could get a glimpse of the mental update in progress. Dream awareness is experienced as a set of sensations that is inconsistent with the sensory reality. Hence, dream awareness shows that the mind is able to create complex sensations without perceiving relative sensory signals. This is further support for the notion that the subconscious constructs the internal reality.

I propose a pragmatic need for dreaming and dream awareness. This does not exclude the possibility that dreams are affected by the extrasensory reality. However, that evaluation is outside the scope of nemonik thinking.

ABSTRACTS OTHER BOOKS

GLOSSARY...

Glossary of Nemonik Thinking (Schade 2016). Nemonik thinking is a competitive advantage because it mobilizes your hidden genius, accelerates your thinking, improves your memory, prevents blind-spots, and reveals opportunities, while its constant preparedness reduces stress levels. Definitions associated with the mind and reality are inherently hypothetical, fuzzy, and intertwined. Nevertheless, to improve our understanding of the way we think, we have to identify, differentiate, and define those components. Therefore, this glossary provides descriptions for the concepts associated with nemonik thinking. To become skilled in nemonik thinking, it is recommended to study—*Think Smarter with Nemonik Thinking (Schade, 2016).*

DICTIONARY...

Dictionary Nemonik Thinking (Schade 2016). Nemonik thinking mobilizes your hidden genius, accelerates your thinking, improves your memory, reveals opportunities and threats, creates questions and ideas, and reduces your stress levels. Nemonik thinking divides the mind into 17 nemonik regions. Those regions defragment information, which facilitates the storage, maintenance, recall, and processing of associated information from memory. However, the boundaries of those nemonik regions are fuzzy. Therefore, the aim of this dictionary is to differentiate them by providing keywords for each nemonik concept. The first part of this dictionary translates nemonik concepts into common keywords (e.g. *advance* into attack, bypass, etc.). In contrast, the second part translates common keywords into nemonik concepts (e.g. attack, bypass, etc. into *advance*). This dictionary shows that the complexity of conventional thinking comprises thousands of keywords that can be simplified to 17 nemoniks. This reduction will increase the speed of your thinking. To become skilled in nemonik thinking, it is recommended to study—*Think Smarter with Nemonik Thinking (Schade, 2016).*

GLOBAL WARMING...

Global Warming is the Solution (Schade 2016). This study presents a bilateral synthesis of artificial global warming and natural global cooling. Mainstream climatology lacks scientific integrity and statistical methodology. Peer review is changed into peer pressure and objectors are labelled '*Deniers*'. Proper statistical analyses are replaced by graphs and non-causal correlation analyses that are based on the last 166 years, while 420,000 years of Antarctic data are mainly discarded. Furthermore, climatology ignores that 400 ppm of CO2 predicts a global temperature of 11.5 °C, rather than the current 1.3 °C. It focuses on artificial global warming and overlooks the threat of natural global cooling. It also ignores the solar expert Professor Zharkova, who predicts a mini ice-age by 2030, which is likely to turn global warming into global cooling. The current study compared the Antarctic temperatures during the last 10,000 years (baseline 0.00 °C) with the global temperature of 1.3 °C. This common definition of global warming failed to reach statistical significance. However, the Antarctic temperatures during the last 420.000 years support the notion that we live in a glacial period of -8.9 °C, rather than in an interglacial period of 0.00 °C. In that case, the artificial global warming would be 10.2 °C, rather than 1.3 °C. This alternative definition of global warming is statistically significant. Furthermore, it is supported by the current CO2 level of 400 ppm and the significant duration and stability of the current interglacial. Consequently, decreasing the CO2 level could cause a global disaster threatening the survival of humanity. The increased thermal range and the precarious balance between artificial global warming and natural global cooling could also explain the current climatological instability.

LAO ZI'S DAO DE JING

Lao Zi's Dao De Jing—The Way (Schade, Planned 2017). In one curt sentence, Lao Zi explains the core of his book—*Use it to obtain what you seek and to escape what you suffer.* His inspirational guideline introduces the sophisticated yet simple principle of Dao. This principle explains the Universe, the meaning of life, and our place in nature. For more than two and a half thousand years, *Dao De Jing* has been shrouded in mystery. Many scholars have studied that intriguing manuscript by peeling away layer after layer of meaning to unravel its cryptic secrets. Nevertheless, this interpretation shows that *Dao De Jing* preserved its ancient secrets within a prosaic collection of aphorisms. These mysteries are revealed for the first time ever in a clearly understandable way, imparting forgotten knowledge about the Universe and the art of living. To become skilled in nemonik thinking, it is recommended to study—*Think Smarter with Nemonik Thinking (Schade, 2016).*

SUN ZI'S THE ART OF WAR

Sun Zi's *Bing Fa—The Art of War (Schade, Planned 2017).* Sun Zi (554-496 BC) was a Chinese warrior-philosopher who wrote the military classic *Bing Fa* or *The Art of War*. Although his book is about war, his strategies apply to every facet of daily life. Sun Zi deals with the art of positioning yourself in space, matter, and time. He addresses the questions raised by nemonik thinking of where, what, and when to advance, stay, retreat, accumulate, preserve, dispose, act, wait, prepare, accept, reject, reveal, and conceal. Think smarter and incorporate Sun Zi's strategies in your thinking. To become skilled in nemonik thinking, it is recommended to study—*Think Smarter with Nemonik Thinking (Schade, 2016).*

COVER DESIGN

The mirror images on the front and back of the cover illustrate the intentional emptiness of this manual. This manual is referred to as *empty* because nemonik thinking is not fostering or inhibiting any cult, doctrine, dogma, ideology, or religion. Nemonik thinking generates questions and ideas, rather than answers or opinions. Responses to those questions and ideas depend on the actual situation and the belief system of the thinker. Nemonik thinking is a neutral mental skill that activates your thinking. It is about how to think, rather than what to believe. Seeing a deeper meaning in it is a clear misunderstanding concerning the essence of nemonik thinking.

DECLARATION OF INDEPENDENCE

I, Dr Auke Schade, declare that this study and the development of nemonik thinking were funded by private resources. No part of this study, or the development of nemonik thinking, was supported, financially or otherwise, by any third party including individuals, stakeholders, charities, commercial, academic, political, ideological, military, religious, and secret organizations. Consequently, I am an independent researcher and do not have to please anyone.

The main global problems are symptoms of humanity's dramatically failing way of thinking. Although a huge and immediate threat, climate change is only one of the many symptoms. Seen the lethargic response of leaders to global warming, it would be unwise to rely on the global establishment for adequate action. Turning the tide in time will require huge sacrifices and resources. Therefore, support from any individual or organisation will be welcomed, as long as it will not comprise my academic integrity.

Now, after the completion of this study and the development of nemonik thinking, I feel even free to approach the oil and coal industries for funding. Confirmation of the bilateral climate-change hypothesis would transform them from villains into heroes. Their industrial CO2 might save us from living on a frozen planet.

Donations Welcome!

WEBSITE

It is the aim of the website *nemonik-thinking.org* to provide interactive on-line information about nemonik thinking. This includes discussions, books, blog, videos, exercises, updates, activities, web links, and tests. Join the nemonik thinkers and receive the latest updates. It is a work in progress. Check it out and have your say! I look forward to your feedback at:

nemonik-thinking.org

SIR RICHARD BRANSON

Sir Richard Branson achieved global recognition as a successful adventurer, airline operator, author, balloonist, billionaire, business magnate, celebrity, editor, entrepreneur, environmentalist, film producer, founder of the Virgin group, humanitarian, investor, music producer, powerboat racer, publisher, etc. He has become a symbol of the inventive and adventurous business approach by showing that it can be fun. His actions feature creativity, initiative, momentum, and speed, while he bypasses obstacles, and avoids counterproductive confrontations. Sir Richard's autobiography—*Losing My Virginity*—is a well-written high-octane narrative of life through the eyes of this maverick.[155] His book is certainly entertaining. It has also been a great source of information for my comparison between Sir Richard's way of thinking and nemonik thinking.

Studying Sir Richard's experiences could save you time and effort by increasing your awareness of the potential strengths, weaknesses, opportunities, and threats of life. His goals might differ, but you could use the same strategies to achieve yours.

Incompetent thinkers do not learn from their actions.
Competent thinkers learn from their actions.
Nemonik thinkers learn from the actions of others.

Email Sir Richard

----- Original Message -----
From: richard
To: auke schade
Sent: Sunday, August 19, 2007 8:08 PM
Subject: Re: Your request for more information

The Plan is excellent, though still some issues with it.
As you already know our company is all about being different, and your idea is certainly that. We will want to take this to the next step.

It will be a little drawn out as business always is, send me some cantact details, and someone will arrange a meeting.
Unfortunately sometimes i cannot always be present, but if that happens a representative of sound experience and guidance will attend.
Kind Regards.

Notes

ENDNOTES

---

[1] The nemonik definitions and keywords can be found in this manual and my books *Glossary for Nemonik Thinking (2016)* and *Dictionary for Nemonik Thinking (2016).*

[2] In Einstein's formula $E = mc^2$: E = energy; m = mass; and c = the speed of light. The formula shows that energy and mass are two sides of the same coin. They are different manifestations of the same phenomenon. The formula also shows that there is a large amount of energy in a small amount of matter.

[3] Schade, A. (Planned 2017). Lao Zi's True Dao De Jing. nemonik-thinking.org.

[4] The 'heart' is a romantic synonym for the subconscious.

[5] Computers might be faster, but it is unlikely that we could design artificial intelligence that thinks fundamentally different. A computer is a reflection of the human mind. Therefore, a computer is a good example to describe the mind.

[6] The internal reality will be discussed in Schade, A. (2017). *The Unreal Reality.*

[7] Lorenz, E. (1963). Deterministic nonperiodic flow. Journal of Atmospheric Sciences, 20, 130-141.

[8] Spencer, In Chalmers Mitchell, Sir P., Materialism and Vitalism in Biology. The Herbert Spencer lecture, 1930, p. 5., 1930.

[9] Spencer, Herbert (1820-1903)—English philosopher who introduced the important distinctions between the *known, unknown, and unknowable.*

[10] Branson, Sir R. (1999), p. 29, 34, 36, 55, 193, 228, 332, and 443.

[11] Schade, A. (Planned 2017). Lao Zi's Principle for Nemonik Thinkers. Chapter 5.

[12] Control; Branson, Sir R. (1999), p. 82 and 90—Chaos; p. 185 and 229—Coutts' bank and the City; p. 208, 209, 233, and 234.

[13] Balloons; Branson, Sir R. (1999), p. 239—Chaotic; p. 239.

[14] Practical numbers; Branson, Sir R. (1999), p. 36—Critical; p. 436 and 438—Compensate; p. 52.

[15] Schade, A. (Planned 2017). Lao Zi's Principle for Nemonik Thinkers. Chapter 71.

[16] Cost; Branson, Sir R. (1999), p. 138, 171, 172, and 255—EMI; p. 254—Virgin Music; p. 255, 398, 407-409, and 472.

[17] Branson, Sir R. (1999), p. 407-409, and 472

[18] Suzuki, D. (1956). *Zen Buddhism.* (W. Barret, Ed.) USA: Doubleday Anchor Books & Hoffmann, Y. (1977). *The Sound of the One Hand. Granada* Publishing Limited.

[19] *Dao* is a phonetic notation of Chinese pictographs and, therefore, it is alternatively spelled as *Tao.*

[20] *De* is a phonetic notation of Chinese pictographs and, therefore, it is alternatively spelled as *Te*. Schade, A. (Planned 2017). Lao Zi's Principle *for Nemonik Thinkers.*

[21] Newton Sir, I. (1687). Philosophiae Naturalis Principia Mathematica (The Mathematical Principles of Natural Philosophy).

[22] Mathematics and root learning; Branson, Sir R. (1999), p. 34 and 55—Distrust of numbers; p. 29, 36, and 193.

[23] Airlines; Branson, Sir R. (1999), p. 196 and 202—Ballooning; p. 2, 3, 238, 239, 268, 278, and 297—Consumables; p. 473—Computer games; p. 263, 470, and 471—Cosmetics; p. 475—Financial Services; p. 439 and 474—Railways; p. 359—Soft drinks; p. 473.

[24] Confucius. (1979). *The Analects.* (B. Radice, Ed., & D. C. Lau, Trans.) Middlesex, England: Penguin Books.

[25] The correct answer would be 2 + 5 x 7 = 2 + (5 x 7) = 2 + 35 = 37. The incorrect answer would be 2 + 5 x 7 = (2 + 5) x 7 = 7 x 7 = 49. The collective has decided arbitrarily to multiply numbers before adding them.

[26] In the past, people removed some of the edges of cold coins. As a result, people collected the undamaged coins and the damaged ones stayed in circulation. Nowadays, this law has a more general application holding that bad things drive out good things.

[27] Schade, A. (Planned 2017). Lao Zi's Principle *for Nemonik Thinkers.* Chapter 38.

[28] Schade, A. (Planned 2017). Lao Zi's Principle *for Nemonik Thinkers.* Chapter 72.

---

[29] Schade, A. (Planned 2017). Lao Zi's Principle *for Nemonik Thinkers.* Chapter 58.

[30] Schade, A. (Planned 2017). Lao Zi's Principle *for Nemonik Thinkers.* Chapter 58.

[31] Schade, A. (Planned 2017). Lao Zi's Principle *for Nemonik Thinkers.* Chapter 57.

[32] da Vinci, Leonardo (1452-1519) was an Italian Renaissance genius who excelled as an anatomist, architect, botanist, cartographer, engineer, geologist, inventor, mathematician, musician, painter, sculptor, and writer. His most famous painting is the Mona Lisa.

[33] Branson, Sir R. (1999), p. 392, 394, 397, 402, and 419.

[34] Ethical standards; Branson, Sir R. (1999), p. 465—Equal application; p. 468—Negotiate contracts; p. 282, 291, and 440.

[35] British Airways; Branson, Sir R. (1999), p. 319, 391, 396, 406, and 448—CAA; p. 320 and 321—European Commission; p. 331—Japanese intergovernmental agreement; p. 250—Monopolies and Mergers Commission; p. 249—Traffic Distribution Rules and Heathrow Slot Committee; p. 326 and 329.

[36] Family; Branson, Sir R. (1999), p. 206 and 354—Friends; p. 68, 72, 176, and 258—Charities; p. 62, 69, 280, 282, 290, and 446—Peace activities; p. 57.

[37] Conception, incubation, and hatching are sometimes considered to be stages of creative thinking.

[38] Alternatively, this strategy is called *Trial and Error.*

---

[39] de Bono, E. (1970). *Lateral Thinking*. New York, USA: Harper & Row, Publishers.

[40] Self-creativity; Branson, Sir R. (1999), p. 435, 441, 442, 459, and 462—Team creativity; p. 259, 388, 440, and 459—Business creativity; p. 436, 440, 441, 442, and 459—Imagination; p. 29—From nowhere; p. 435—Notebook; p. 171, 441, 442, and 466.

[41] Virgin Airways; Branson, Sir R. (1999), p. 163—Nik Powell; p. 67 and 68.

[42] External creativity; Branson, Sir R. (1999), p. 442—Atlantic airline; p. 192—Paris Megastore; p. 256—British trains; p. 358—Virgin Cola; p. 436—Financial-services; p. 439—Virgin Atlantic; p. 431.

[43] Intuition; Branson, Sir R. (1999), p. 29, 34, 36, 55, 193, 228, 332, and 443—Impulses; p. 13—Decisions people; p. 145 and 151—Decisions issues; p. 193 and 234—Chaos; p. 185 and 229—Formality; p. 344 and 441.

[44] Rumours; Branson, Sir R. (1999), p. 174—Event Magazine; p. 182—Rolling Stones; p. 387—Janet Jackson; p. 332—Trains; p. 358.

[45] Virgin's flotation; Branson, Sir R. (1999), p. 228, 233, 253, and 471—MCEG; p. 192—CD factory; p. 259 and 260.

[46] Branson, Sir R. (1999), p. 12, 213, 326, and 469.

[47] Schade, A. (Planned 2017). Lao Zi's Principle *for Nemonik Thinkers*. Chapter 71.

[48] Branson, Sir R. (1999), p. 52, 168, 189, and 196.

[49] Determination; Branson, Sir R. (1999), p. 52, 174, 190, 194, 195, 220, 253, 257, 334, 336, 350, 407, 408, 409, 434, 437, and 444—Competition; p. 26, 462, 463, 468, and 469—Challenges; p. 11, 12, 195, 213, and 220.

[50] Positive attitude; Branson, Sir R. (1999), p. 68, 138, 208, 258, and 463—Stagnation; p. 467.

[51] Zen Buddhism—school of Buddhism that developed in China and spread later to Japan. The aim of Zen is to see the world as it is. Live in the now and here. The ultimate state of nirvana can be reached in a single lifetime, rather than in a succession of value accumulating lives.

[52] Freud, Sigmund (1856-1939)—pioneer of Western psychology who introduced the psychoanalysis of the subconscious.

[53] Aristotle (~384-322 BC)—a Greek philosopher who developed the validity rules for reason, which form the basis for rational thinking.

[54] Lao Zi (~6th c. BC)—a Chinese philosopher who, about two-and-half thousand years ago, wrote the book *Dao De Jing*. Lao Zi was one of the first philosophers who made a distinction between objective and collective thinking.

[55] Lao Zi (~6th c. BC)—a Chinese philosopher who, about two-and-half thousand years ago, wrote the book *Dao De Jing*. Lao Zi was one of the first philosophers who made a distinction between objective and collective thinking.

[56] Spencer, H. (1930). In Chalmers Mitchell, Sir P., Materialism and Vitalism in Biology. The Herbert Spencer lecture, 1930, p. 5. Claredon Press.

---

[57] Newton, Sir Isaac (1642-1727)—a British mathematician, physicists who described in his book—*Principia*—some of the basic laws of nature.

[58] Confucius (551-479 BC)—a Chinese philosopher who was one of the first to address the problems concerning the artificial rules of collectives.

[59] de Bono, Edward (1933--)—a Maltese consultant, inventor, and physician who introduced lateral thinking in 1970.

[60] Lao Zi (~6th c. BC)—a Chinese philosopher who, about two-and-half thousand years ago, wrote the book *Dao De Jing*. Lao Zi was one of the first philosophers who made a distinction between objective and collective thinking.

[61] Spencer, Herbert (1820-1903)—English philosopher who introduced the important distinctions between the *known, unknown, and unknowable*.

[62] Schade, A. (planned 2017). The Unreal Reality.

[63] Gribben, J. (1999). *Get a Grip on New Physics*. London, UK: Weidenfield and Nicolson, p. 67.

[64] Kaku, M. (1994). *Hyperspace*. New York: Oxford University Press, Inc., p. 173.

[65] William Shakespeare's play—Richard III.

[66] Foot, I. C. (Ed.). (1995). *The Oxford Companion to the Second World War. Oxford:* Oxford University Press, p. 109.

[67] Advance; Branson, Sir R. (1999), p. 180 and 441—Student Magazine; p. 470—Global enterprise; p. 188, 470-475—

EMI; p. 235—Janet Jackson; p. 334—Rolling Stones; p. 387—Rumours; p. 174.

[68] Advance; Branson, Sir R. (1999), p. 138, 173, 175, 180, 190, 235, 250, 261, 332, 358, and 441—Competitive; p. 26, 462, 463, 468, and 469—Determination; p. 52, 174, 190, 194, 195, 220, 253, 257, 334, 336, 350, 407, 409, 434, 437, and 444—Student Magazine; p. 69—Mail-order; p. 73—Janet Jackson; p. 333 and 334—Rolling Stones; p. 387.

[69] Confrontations; Branson, Sir R. (1999), p. 68, 138, 208, 258, 395, 402, and 463—Nik Powell; p. 174 and 175—Don Cruickshank; p. 253—Entire board; p. 257—Nova Scotia; p. 336.

[70] Schade, A. (planned 2017). Sun Zi's Strategies for Nemonik Thinkers.

[71] Coutts Bank; Branson, Sir R. (1999), p. 208 and 228—Nova Scotia Bank; p. 252 and 333—Lloyds Bank; p. 275, 313, 315, 338, 397, and 409.

[72] Retreat; Branson, Sir R. (1999), p. 409 and 412—Event Magazine; p. 182—Management buyout; p. 471—EMI; p. 254—Virgin Music; p. 255, 398, 407, 408, 409, 412, and 472.

[73] Branson, Sir R. (1999), p. 444 and 474.

[74] The gambler advises—*Know when to hold (preserve), and know when to fold, walk, and run (dispose).* In most card games you do not have a choice in the accumulation. The cards are distributed randomly. In real life, you have also to know what to accumulate and what not. It is a choice! The gambler could not maximize his success because he ignored that missing nemonik. He suffered from a mental

blind-spot and, therefore, he broke only even. The morale—nemonik thinking applies even to gambling!

[75] Schade, A. (planned 2017). Lao Zi's Principle *for Nemonik Thinkers*. Chapter 9.

[76] Competition; Branson, Sir R. (1999), p. 26, 462, 463, 468, and 469—Home-grown; p. 444 and 465—Reinvested; p. 137, 228, 314, and 332—Bank loans; p. 199, 209, 210, 228, 252, 254, 275, 313, 315, 333, 338, 350, 352, 396, 397, and 409—Virgin's flotation; p. 228, 229, 233, and 235—Joint-ventures; p. 192, 261, 263, 266, 267, 359, 439, 440, and 475.

[77] Attitude; Branson, Sir R. (1999), p. 208—Avoiding conflicts; p. 68, 138, 208, 258, 395, 402, and 463—No grudges; p. 72, 190, 258, and 395—Sharing success; p. 206 and 354.

[78] Employees are first priority; Branson, Sir R. (1999), p. 175, 462, 463, and 465—Right people; p. 437 and 443—Delegate; p. 464—Accountability; p. 321—Personal contact; p. 321, 463, and 464—Motivate; p. 259, 388, and 411—Praise; p. 68 and 463—Promotions; p. 464—Second changes; p. 72, 190, 258, 259, 388, 395, and 411—Experts; p. 52, 168, 189, and 196.

[79] Good deal; Branson, Sir R. (1999), p. 462 and 465—Supplier loyalty; p. 464—Protect investors; p. 235, 253, and 465.

[80] Student Magazine; Branson, Sir R. (1999), p. 40, 45, and 470—Airlines; p. 163 and 470—Airship advertising; p. 472—Brand-consultancy; p. 473—Communications; p. 470, 471, 472, and 473—Consumables; p. 473—Computer games; p. 263, 470, and 471—Cosmetics; p. 475—Film

studio; p. 190—Financial services; p. 439 and 474—Holiday provider; p. 210 and 470—Mail-order; p. 69 and 470—Megastores; p. 256 and 257—Necker Island; p. 163—Nightclubs; p. 166 and 470—Publishing house; p. 166 and 472—Railways; p. 359 and 474—Record label; p. 110 and 470—Recording studio, p. 79 and 470—Retail shops; p. 73, 470, and 474—Soft drinks; p. 436 and 473.

[81] Hawking, S. (1998). *A Brief History of Time.* Great Britain: Bantam Press.

[82] Stagnation; Branson, Sir R. (1999), p. 468—People; p. 175, 258, 437, 443, 462, 463, 464, and 465—Preserve; p. 72, 190, 258, 259, 388, 395, and 411.

[83] Cash-flow; Branson, Sir R. (1999), p. 332—Overextension; p. 180, 208, 228, 252, 313, 315, 333, 338, 352, and 397—Fired; p. 138, 171, and 172.

[84] Branson, Sir R. (1999), p. 464.

[85] Branson, Sir R. (1999), p. 253.

[86] Branson, Sir R. (1999), p. 192.

[87] IPC; Branson, Sir R. (1999), p. 71 and 435—Event Magazine; p. 182—Sega licence; p. 338—Virgin Vision; p. 472—EMI; p. 255, 398, 407-409, 412, and 472.

[88] Branson, Sir R. (1999), p. 138, 171, 172, and 255.

[89] Dispose employees; Branson, Sir R. (1999), p. 138 and 172—Dispose artists; p. 138 and 172.

[90] Dispose Nik Powell; Branson, Sir R. (1999), p. 67 and 68—Inviting Nik back; p. 72—Nik's inabilities; p. 172, 175, and 209—Nik's split-up; p. 176.

[91] Branson, Sir R. (1999), p. 200 and 201.

[92] Nemonik thinking is exhaustive and, therefore, the possible actions are determined by the remaining nemoniks—*accept, accumulate, advance, conceal, dispose, prepare, preserve, reject, retreat, reveal, stay, and wait.* The keywords include also some synonyms for act—*carry out, create, do, execute, go, memorize, move, perform, react, recall, respond, and rule.*

[93] Schade, A. (planned 2017). Lao Zi's Principle *for Nemonik Thinkers.* Chapter 8.

[94] Schade, A. (planned 2017). Sun Zi's Strategies for Nemonik Thinkers.

[95] Present; Branson, Sir R. (1999), p. 409—Past; p. 413 and 441—Future; p. 409.

[96] Branson, Sir R. (1999), p. 67, 68, 145, 151, 169, 193, and 234.

[97] Student Magazine and the Student Advisory Centre; Branson, Sir R. (1999), p. 69—Mail-order; p. 73—Event Magazine; p. 182—EMI; p. 254—Virgin Music; p. 255, 398, 407, 408, 409, 412, and 472.

[98] Branson, Sir R. (1999), p. 338.

[99] Branson, Sir R. (1999), p. 410.

[100] Determination; p. 52, 174, 175, 190, 194, 195, 253, 257, 334, 336, 350, 407-409, 434, 437, and 444—Priorities; p. 387, 434, and 462—Intuition; p. 29, 193, 228, and 332—Impulses; p. 13, 234, 239, and 441—Momentum; p. 180 and 441.

---

[101] Virgin Music; Branson, Sir R. (1999), p. 351, 390, 408, 409, and 412—British Airways; p. 392, 394, 395, 397, 402, and 419.

[102] Branson, Sir R. (1999), p. 412.

[103] Branson, Sir R. (1999), p. 192.

[104] Schade, A. (planned 2017). Sun Zi's Strategies for Nemonik Thinkers.

[105] Nemonik thinking is not a cure for mental illness. For such problems, seek advice of a healthcare professional.

[106] Some argue that the past is gone and the future has not arrived yet. Therefore, they advise us to live in the present or the NOW. However, time is a continuum that people divide in artificial units of measurement such as years, days, hours, minutes, etc. There are no such real separations in the continuum of time and, therefore, we cannot identify a natural unit that we could call the present. Hence, the present is also an artificial concept. What we perceive as the present is a period of time that is not infinitely small. If I would perceive an infinitely small present, then I would perceive neither time nor movement. For example, I cannot see the wings of a bumble bee in flight. It is just a blur of movement that is created by past and present positions of the wings. Past and present are intertwined to create the perception of movement. If my mind could reduce the duration of the perceived present, then I would be able to freeze the blur and see a sharp picture of those wings. This effect is shown by fast cameras that record a shorter present than the one I experience. Those pictures are able to freeze the wings in time. Hence, in my reality I cannot separate past and present. Another exam-

ple is our speech. The words that we utter in the present are learned in the past. Even in our speech, the past and present become one. Consequently, I cannot live purely in the present, because I would be unable to speak. Furthermore, if I shoot an arrow or drive a car, then I have to anticipate the future. Otherwise, the arrow would not hit the target and my car would hit a concrete wall. Hence, it is static and counterproductive to pretend that we can live in the present by excluding the past and future. In contrast, nemonik thinkers are dynamic and focus on the past, present, or future as required by the actual situation.

[107] Nemonik thinking is not a cure for mental illnesses. For such problems, seek advice of a healthcare professional.

[108] Reasonable standard = 5 x 80% = 400%.

[109] Branson, Sir R. (1999), p. 213.

[110] Adaptation; Branson, Sir R. (1999), p. 259, 388, and 436—Competition; p. 26, 462, 463, 468, and 469—Fair play; p. 322, 329, 428, 447, 462, 463, 465, 468, and 469—Forgiveness; p. 72, 190, 258, and 395—Honesty; p. 137, 182, 235, 253, 447, and 448—Independence; p. 82, 90, 146, 234, and 438—Praise; p. 68 and 463—Reputation; p. 90, 253, 419, 438, 444-446, and 448.

[111] Macro leadership; Branson, Sir R. (1999), p. 440 and 464—Priorities; p. 171, 332, 387, 433, 434, and 462—Delegation; p. 464—Accountability; p. 321—Overall control; p. 82 and 90.

[112] Listening; Branson, Sir R. (1999), p. 442, 463, and 464—Decisive; p. 67, 68, 145, 151, 169, 193, and 234—Sticks to decisions; p. 52, 174, 190, 194, 195, 220, 253, 257, 334, 336, 350, 407, 409, 434, 437, and 444.

[113] Flat hierarchy of small symbiotic units; Branson, Sir R. (1999), p. 444 and 464—Employees first; p. 175, 258, 437, 443, 462, and 463-465—Open-door policy; p. 321, 463, and 464—Teamwork; p. 72, 206, 258, 321, 354, 440, 443, 463, and 465.

[114] No confrontations; Branson, Sir R. (1999), p. 68, 138, 208, 258, 395, 402, and 463—Bypasses; p. 175, 253, 257, and 336—Delegates disposal; p. 138—Avoids court action; p. 392, 394, 395, 397, 402, and 419.

[115] Branson, Sir R. (1999), p. 444, 445, 462-465, and 469.

[116] Goals long-term; Branson, Sir R. (1999), p. 283 and 472—Challenging; p. 11, 12, 195, 213, 215, and 440—Creative; p. 29, 259, 388, 435, 440, 441, 442, 459, 462, and 466—Survival; p. 12 and 433—Idealist; p. 435—Not just money; p. 53, 69, and 446—Humanitarian efforts; p. 62, 69, 280, 282, 290, 446.

[117] Translating ideas in plans; Branson, Sir R. (1999), p. 71, 165, 435, 437, 443, and 462—Strong focus; p. 434—Intuitive; p. 29, 34, 36, 55, 193, 228, 332, and 443—Impulsive; p. 13—People; p. 145 and 151—Issues; p. 193, 228, and 234.

[118] Janet Jackson; Branson, Sir R. (1999), p. 333 and 334—Rolling Stones; p. 387.

[119] People oriented; Branson, Sir R. (1999), p. 175, 258, 437, 462, 463-465—Organic structure; p. 444, 445, 462-465, and 469—Small independent units; p. 444, 462, 464, and 469—Symbiosis; p. 443—Vertical integration; p. 165, 190, and 260—Joint-ventures; p. 192, 261, 263, 264, 266, 267, 359, 439, 440, and 475—Open communication; p. 321, 463, and 464—Variety of markets; p. 180, 435, and 444.

[120] EMI; Branson, Sir R. (1999), p. 235—British Airways; p. 367 and 424—Employees and board; p. 174, 175, 253, and 257—Saddam Hussein; p. 282 and 291—Balloon to Miyakonojo; p. 268—Splitting up the Virgin group; p. 210—Relocation of programmers; p. 340.

[121] Branson, Sir R. (1999), p. 68, 138, 208, 258, 395, 402, and 463.

[122] Cash-flow control; Branson, Sir R. (1999), p. 260 and 332—Cost control; p. 138, 171, 172, 255, 332—Cutting losses; p. 182, 254, and 409—Geographical spread; p. 192, 235, 250, 256, 257, 261, 263, 264, 267, and 472—Joint-ventures; p. 192, 261, 263, 264, 266, 267, 359, 439, 440, and 475—Limiting the downside; p. 193, 332, 392, 438, and 443—Mutually protected units; p. 443—Product diversification; p. 188, and 470-475—Independent units; p. 182, 195, 210, 340, 444, 462, 464, and 469—Symbiosis; p. 443.

[123] Branson, Sir R. (1999), p. 138, 173, 175, 180, 190, 235, 250, 261, 332, 358, and 441—Short-term cash-flow; p. 228, 254, 255, 314, and 332—Coutts Bank; p. 208, 209, and 228—Nova Scotia Bank; p. 252 and 333—Lloyds Bank; p. 275, 313, 315, 338, 352, 397, 400, and 409.

[124] EMI; Branson, Sir R. (1999), p. 254—Virgin Music; p. 407-409, and 472—MCEG; p. 192.

[125] Branson, Sir R. (1999), p. 12 and 433.

[126] Branson, Sir R. (1999), p. 321, 463, and 464.

[127] Randolph Fields; Branson, Sir R. (1999), p. 192—Prince Rupert; p. 387—Gerry Spencer; p. 436—Rowan Gormley; p. 439—Chris Hutchins; p. 367—Investigations; p. 424.

[128] Branson, Sir R. (1999), p. 413, 414, and 416.

[129] MCEG; Branson, Sir R. (1999), p. 192—Publishing house; p. 189.

[130] Filmmaking; Branson, Sir R. (1999), p. 190—Virgin Atlantic; p. 195 and 350—Rolling Stones; p. 387—Virgin Music; p. 390 and 408—Flotation of Virgin; p. 228—Management buyout; p. 253—Virgin brand-name; p. 437—Lloyds Insurance; p. 442—Private detectives; p. 322 and 428.

[131] Branson, Sir R. (1999), p. 442.

[132] Promotional skills; Branson, Sir R. (1999), p. 2, 148, 215, 216, 220, 239, 268, 278, 290, 297, and 344—Balloon flights; p. 2, 3, 238, 239, 268, 278, and 297—Powerboat races; p. 215, 216, and 220—Dressing up; p. 343 and 344.

[133] Branson, Sir R. (1999), p. 480-488.

[134] IPC; Branson, Sir R. (1999), p. 71 and 435—Mike Oldfield; p. 137—British Airways; p. 381, 395, 396, and 402

[135] Branson, Sir R. (1999), p. 169.

[136] Branson, Sir R. (1999), p. 68, 138, 208, 258, 395, 402, and 463.

[137] Nightclubs; Branson, Sir R. (1999), p. 174 and 175—Management buyout; p. 253—Megastore; p. 257—Virgin Music; p. 409 and 411.

[138] Employees first; Branson, Sir R. (1999), p. 175, 258, 437, 443, 462, and 463-465—Open-door; p. 321, 463 and

464—Teamwork; p. 72, 206, 258, 321, 354, 440, 443, and 463-465.

[139] Branson, Sir R. (1999), p. 411.

[140] Rumours; Branson, Sir R. (1999), p. 174—Julien Clerc; p. 169—British Airways; p. 367 and 424.

[141] (13 operational nemoniks) x (4 mindmodes) = 52 options.

[142] (13 operational nemoniks) x (4 SWOT components) = 52 options.

[143] (13 operational nemoniks) x (4 mindmodes) x (4 SWOT components) = 208 options.

[144] Nemonik thinking is not a cure for mental illnesses. For such problems, seek advice of a healthcare professional.

[145] Schade, A. (Planned 2017). The Unreal Reality.

[146] Schade, 1995.

[147] Masada is an ancient fortification on the top of a mountain in the Judean desert of Israel. In 73 CE, the Romans laid siege to Masada by surrounding it. They built a ramp against the mountain to take the fortress. The 960 inhabitants had set the storehouses ablaze and committed suicide.

[148] Schade, A. (Planned 2017). Sun Zi's Strategies for Nemonik Thinkers.

[149] Sir Isaac Newton (1642-1727)—British scientist who explained most of traditional physics in his book *Philosophiae Naturalis Principia Mathematica* (Gribben, 1999, p. 8).

[150] Gribben, J. (1999). *Get a Grip on New Physics.* London, UK: Weidenfield and Nicolson, p. 29.

[151] Thomas Young (1773-1829)—showed that light moves through space like a wave (Gribben, 1999, pp. 28-30).

[152] Gribben, J. (1999). *Get a Grip on New Physics.* London, UK: Weidenfield and Nicolson, p. 84.

[153] Schade, A. (2016). Global Warming is the Solution... nemonik-thinking.org.

[154] Schade, A. (Planned 2017). Sun Zi's Strategies for Nemonik Thinkers.

[155] Branson, Sir R. (1999). *Losing my Virginity: The Autobiography.* Australia: Random House Australia.

www.ingramcontent.com/pod-product-compliance
Lightning Source LLC
Chambersburg PA
CBHW050109280326
41933CB00010B/1026